FINALLY BECOMING HER

finally Becoming Her

The 6-Month Transformation Journal
To Create A Life You´re Obsessed with &
Become The Most Empowered Version Of Yourself

Kathrine Louis

Publishing:
BoD · Books on Demand GmbH, In de Tarpen 42, 22848 Norderstedt, bod@bod.de
Print: Libri Plureos GmbH, Friedensallee 273, 22763 Hamburg

ISBN: 978-3-7693-2815-8

THIS BOOK IS DEDICATED TO:

To my three beautiful and gorgeous children, whom I still call and refer to (and always will) as my babies! You are my greatest and most beautiful source of inspiration, the driving force within me that keeps me going and pushing forward.

You are so incredibly talented, and all I want for you is to fully embrace your amazing power and gifts.
It won't always be easy—but it will always be worth it.
And Mama will always and forever be right by your side, having your back.

You deserve all the love and magical blessings this earth has to offer. You deserve the world, and I will do it all for you. The world is yours!

I love you to the moon and back—and through the entire universe!

Always and forever,
Mama

CONTENTS

INTRODUCTION

This is probably one of the most important first pages you will read in your life. And yes, I know I'm setting the bar high.

In my 42 years on this planet, I've learned and experienced a few things that I know for certain:

- You Can. And You Will absolutely be, do, create, and achieve anything you want in your life. It's not only your birthright to be happy and fulfilled, but also to shine your light brightly while living in your purpose. Let me help you get there!
- Everything in your life so far—the good, the bad, and the ugly—has, in some shape or form, prepared you for what you desire most. Your soul has chosen this path, and yes, I know that can be a tough one to understand.
- Even if it is difficult to understand right now, the way you experience life is deeply tied to your self-worth. Whether you believe you deserve something or not, your experiences will reflect that belief.
- Believe in yourself and never give up on your dreams! You literally owe it to yourself. Your life is to be lived, and every single day is so precious!

You are your single biggest and most important bet. You should always be your most valuable asset. Treat yourself as such and be mindfule of your self worth. So, keep going. You deserve all of this!

Here is the key to achieving any kind of success: You need to consistently focus on your goals, which will inevitably lead to taking aligned actions.

This will, in turn, program your subconscious mind to believe that you have everything it takes to reach those goals. Your self-worth will begin to reflect this newfound confidence.

If, deep down, you believe that you don't deserve your goals, you will subconsciously push them away and sabotage your efforts. Sounds wild, right? But here's the truth: 95% of all decisions and actions you take are driven by your subconscious mind.
That's why personal transformation and self-improvement work are so important.

I designed "Finally Becoming Her" specifically to provide the consistency you need—without you having to take extra steps or re-buy after just a few weeks. Every single transformative journaling technique, as well as the daily reflections, is built on the foundation of my coaching method, {The East Hampton Method}, which has helped my clients experience massive, life-changing transformations.

And yes, falling off the bandwagon or becoming inconsistent is expected. It's not failure—it's life. When it happens, just get back on track. Don't give inconsistency the power to stop you from achieving your goals.

trust *the* PROCESS

THIS JOURNAL IS FOR YOU IF:

- You currently feel stuck and disempowered

- You really want to be more focused on your goals, desires, and dreams—and actually achieve them

- You want to strengthen your intuition and become the most empowered version of yourself

- You want to increase your self-worth

- You want to boost your confidence and experience true self-empowerment

- You are struggling with your mental health and want to experience happier times

- You want to create a life you're truly obsessed with

current vibe:
WORKING FOR
THE LIFESTYLE
I PROMISED TO MYSELF.

HOW THIS JOURNAL WORKS:

The "Finally Becoming Her" 6-Months Personal Transformation Journal is designed to adapt to your personal pace. You can work through it as fast or as slow as you need to, depending on where you are in life right now. Remember, life doesn't always unfold as we intend—things happen, and that's why it was important for me to design a journal that adjusts to your unique situation while still offering daily consistency.

That's the essence of my coaching method, {The East Hampton Method}: It's focused entirely on you. My goal is to help you on your Self-Improvement Journey, supporting you in achieving your goals and dreams in a way that works for your personal transformation. There's no one-size-fits-all solution, and that's what sets my coaching approach apart. This is reflected in the mindset mastery and confidence building results my clients achieve.

You'll find transformative journaling techniques on the following pages that you can either work through one by one or skip for now, starting instead with the daily journaling section and returning to the specific techniques when it feels right for you.

This journal is a 6-month transformation guide that will support your personal development as you set new goals and work toward becoming your best self. One important thing to understand about your transformation is that your goals may change, and that's okay. As you grow and evolve, not only will your perspective on certain topics shift over the next 6 months, but so will your desires and dreams. That's a sign of growth! I'm sharing this with you upfront so that, when you notice these changes, you won't feel insecure. Instead, you'll understand that these shifts are a blessing and a natural part of being serious about your self-development.

You'll find instructions for each Finally Becoming Her journaling technique before each journal section. At the end of the day, it all comes down to you. I'm thrilled to provide you with my most transformative and powerful tools, offering my help and guidance along the way, but ultimately, you are the one putting in the work. And that's the only way it can truly work—because we are talking about your goals, your desires, and your life. You hold that power, and you should never give it away.

Remember, the key to unlocking your potential and manifesting your dream life is staying committed to your personal transformation journey. If you love a particular transformative journaling technique, don't hesitate to share it with your friends and family on social media! Tag me @TheKathrineLouis so I can celebrate your achievements and share the love. I'll be so proud of your accomplishments!

Be your favorite kind of woman.

THE BIGGEST SECRET TO TRANSFORMATION:

Let me share with you the biggest secret to transformation!

Let me tell you the real difference between people who achieve their goals, feel happy and fulfilled, and live their dream lives—and those who struggle to make ends meet.

The secret to success (or the lack thereof) is this: what you believe to be true. Your mindset.

Do you believe you can do it? So be it.
Do you believe you won't achieve your goals? So be it.

We tend to underestimate the power of our beliefs and mindset—because we can't touch it! As human beings, we tend to value things that are tangible—things we can touch, feel, or see, like gold. But what's most important for everything we will experience in life —our beliefs—can't be touched. It is our thoughts and emotions that determine the actions we take.

So here's the biggest secret to it all, the real key to your personal transformation:
Your beliefs will determine your behavior. Your behavior affects the decisions you make and the actions you take. Those actions will determine what you experience as a consequence. And whatever you experience will trigger emotions, which will inevitably confirm your beliefs—whether they're good or bad. Do you see how this forms a circle?

Let me give you an example: Let's say you have a specific goal, but deep down, your subconscious belief is that you're not worth it. As a result, you either don't take action toward that goal, or you try once or twice but give up as soon as you hit a hurdle. This creates an experience of "not working out", which makes you feel like a failure. And guess what? That feeling of failure confirms your belief that you're not worth it.

So, in order to experience real transformation, yes, you're right, we will be working on your beliefs!

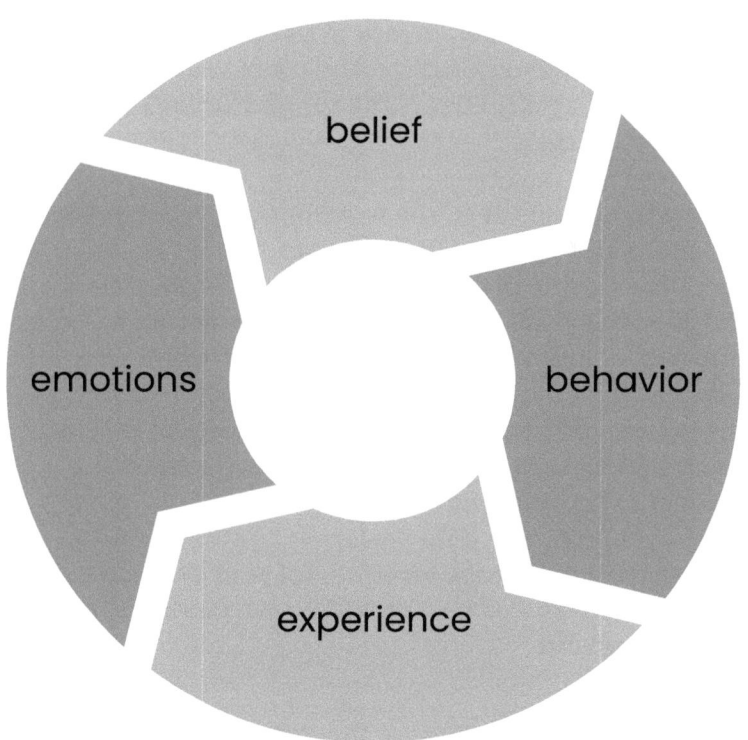

YOUR CURRENT SELF VS. YOUR REINVENTED SELF

This first practice is a fun yet deep one—and also very important because it sets the tone for your future self. Literally.

In order to grow and expand, you need to know where you're starting and what you're working with. Even though I fully understand that digging deep into what you resist or want to move away from can be painful, it's inevitable in order to gain the clarity you need. And believe me—you'll be surprised. The revelations you'll gain during this practice will reveal things you probably haven't been aware of before—and that's exactly what we're going for. The more willing you are to be honest and go deep, the more amazing the outcome will be.

On the first pages, feel free to write down your entire life! Literally! Take your time to write it all down: the good, the bad, and the ugly. And don't forget the things you actually love and want to maintain or improve. Unless you plan to show it to anyone else (which I don't recommend), the only person reading this will be you—so get ready to be frank. Sometimes, being honest and coming clean with yourself is the hardest thing, and that's OK.

Next, I'll ask you to take inventory of your physical environment as well as write down a typical day in your current life.

And now, we get to the fun part! It's time to reinvent yourself!

I want you to go big—no matter how scary that might feel at first. If it doesn't make you overly excited and give you sweaty hands, it's out! I want you to write down all the big, scary dreams you've been secretly wishing for your entire life. I've included some extra prompts to help guide you through this process.

Here's a little secret: When you dream it and desire it in your heart, it's already part of you. So don't hide it any longer—write it down!

Also, write down how you want your physical environment to look and how you'd love your ideal day to unfold. You've probably heard the saying, "Build a life you don't need a vacation from." That's the vibe we're going for. Minus the postcard.

So, let's get ready!

embrace
THE DISCOMFORT,
because that's
WHERE THE MAGIC HAPPENS

YOUR CURRENT SELF / LIFE

describe your current life. what are the key aspects
that define it, and how do they make you feel?

....

....

....

....

....

....

....

....

....

....

....

....

....

....

....

....

....

....

YOUR CURRENT SELF / LIFE

list all the areas of your life you'd like to improve. what changes would help you become your best and most powerful self?

....

....

....

....

....

....

....

....

....

....

....

....

....

....

....

....

....

YOUR CURRENT SELF / LIFE

what are the things you love about your life that you
want to keep and nurture? why do they bring you joy?

TAKE INVENTORY:

describe your physical environment

....

....

....

....

describe a day in your current life, am to pm

am	pm

WHO IS YOUR FUTURE SELF/ BEST VERSION?

IT´S TIME TO REINVENT YOURSELF!

list all the activities that truly light you up—where time disappears and you feel fully alive. how can you create more of these powerful, joyful moments in your everyday life?

....

....

....

....

....

....

....

....

....

....

....

....

....

....

....

WHO IS YOUR FUTURE SELF/ BEST VERSION?

IT´S TIME TO REINVENT YOURSELF!

....

....

....

....

....

....

....

....

....

....

....

....

....

....

....

....

....

WHO IS YOUR FUTURE SELF/ BEST VERSION?

IT´S TIME TO REINVENT YOURSELF!

what makes her/him truly successful? what empowering habits does she/he practice daily, and what mindset fuels her/his unstoppable drive toward greatness?

....

....

....

....

....

....

....

....

....

....

....

....

....

....

....

....

WHO IS YOUR FUTURE SELF/ BEST VERSION?

IT´S TIME TO REINVENT YOURSELF!

....

....

....

....

....

....

....

....

....

....

....

....

....

....

....

....

LET´S REINVENT:
your physical environment

....

....

....

....

---

your future self/ best version day in a life

am	pm

LET´S GET TO IT!

Now it's time to focus on what you truly desire and prioritize for the next 6 months.

It doesn't matter when you start—you can begin in May, July, October, or any other month. What's important is simply that you start. That's why "Finally Becoming Her" is without specific dates, so you can begin on any day of the 6-month journey.

One of the most powerful things I've learned is the practice of choosing a word of intention for the next 6 months. It's like setting a theme for this season of your life.

Remember, life happens in seasons. There are seasons of growth, seasons of letting go, seasons of happiness, and more. But now, you get to choose what you want to focus on in this particular season. The first time I did this practice, I chose the word "surrender." Oh boy, that was a powerful one!

So, what is your word of intention for the next 6 months?

Next, we'll set our goals for the 6 main areas of your life. I chose Self-Care & Wellness, Career & Business, Finance, Family & Friends, Physical Environment, and Self-Development. These 6 areas tend to be the most important to many of us, though of course, we all have different priorities. Feel free to swap any areas to suit your personal needs.

And now, here's the important part: when you're setting your goals, go big! Don't hold back. The only limit you have is the one you set for yourself, so allow yourself to dream bigger than you've ever dreamed before. What's the point of playing small when you have this one precious life to live?

Remember, big goals may feel overwhelming at first, but that's exactly why they're powerful. The excitement and even fear you feel are signs that you're pushing yourself beyond your comfort zone and into real growth. You deserve to set goals that will truly transform your life, and if it makes you nervous—that's a good thing! It means you're on the right path.

So, don't hold back. Be bold, be daring, and set the goals that will bring you closer to the life you've always envisioned for yourself. Your future self is counting on you to dream big!

Make it happen.
SHOCK EVERYONE.

your word of intention for next 6 months: _____

your goals you want to focus on in these 6 main areas:

self care & wellness	career & business
finance	family & friends
physical environment	self development

LET´S TAKE INVENTORY!

Now that we are clear on the goals we're going to focus on and have chosen a word of intention for the next 6 months, it's time to take an inventory.

Why?
Well, it's necessary to know where you're starting. It's crucial to reflect so that you know what to work on and where to begin. If you start without taking an inventory, it can soon feel like you're floating around, kind of directionless, because you won't know where you started or what to improve.

Taking inventory provides clarity and helps you feel empowered to make the right changes—and that's exactly what we're here for.

This Wheel of Life exercise works as follows: color it to the extent that you feel secure, confident, or accomplished in a specific area, starting from the center. The further you reach the outside line, the more you feel confident and in control of that area.

Here's the fun part—and why I recommend using a different color for each area: we'll repeat this exercise every month so you can visibly track your progress and see how far you've come. Sometimes, certain areas may seem to decline before they pick up again, and that's okay! It's a natural part of life. Growth isn't always linear, but each step forward is a step toward becoming your best self.

After 6 months, you'll be able to see your progress and personal transformation in these wheels, which will show you just how much you've grown. So, enjoy the process! This is a marathon, not a race, and your journey to becoming the most empowered version of yourself is worth every step.

Let's begin this exciting chapter of your self-improvement journey!

6 MONTHS OF FOCUSED EFFORT AND ALIGNMENT CAN PUT YOU 5 YEARS AHEAD.

Steven Bartlett

INVENTORY:

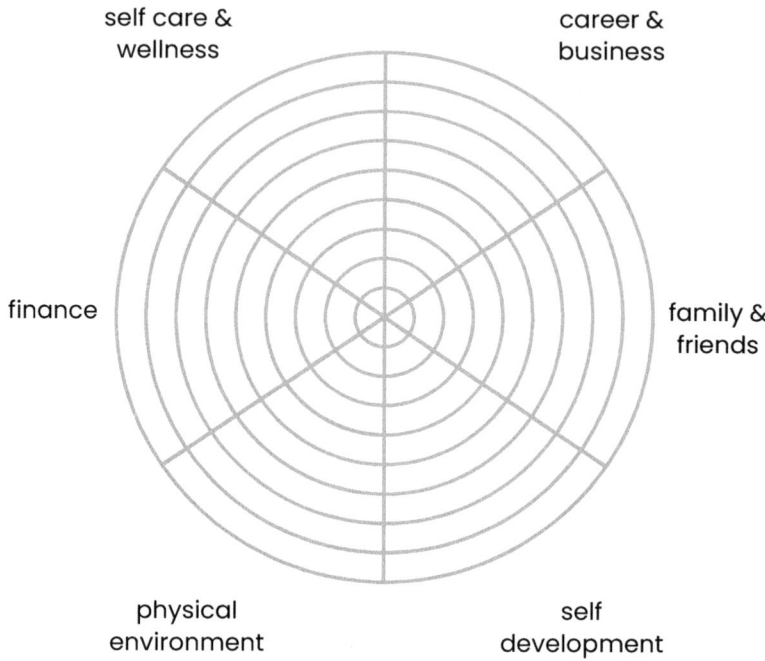

self care & wellness

career & business

finance

family & friends

physical environment

self development

On the following pages, you'll have space to dive deeper into each area of your life. The more honest you are with yourself, the more clarity and transformation you'll experience.
Remember, true growth happens when you allow yourself to be fully open.

self care & wellness

....

....

....

....

....

....

career & business

....

....

....

....

....

....

finance

....

....

....

....

....

family & friends

....

....

....

....

....

....

physical environment

....

....

....

....

....

....

self development

....

....

....

....

....

ENERGY TAKERS VS. ENERY GIVERS

Ok, so this is a biggie:
We tend to quickly label ourselves as "too sensitive" when a situation—or especially a person—makes us feel a certain way. You know that feeling when meeting someone or dealing with a specific situation leaves you feeling drained or exhausted?

Here's my professional advice: believe it!
Your emotions don't lie. Energy doesn't lie. Never.

If something is draining your energy, it's a signal that shouldn't be ignored. Energy awareness is essential for your personal transformation. I need you to become fully aware of the people or situations that drain your energy—and on the positive side, what gives you energy and makes you feel empowered.

Being aware of both will allow you to:
A) Balance your energy more effectively, and
B) Avoid, as much as possible, those energy drainers that prevent you from being your best self.

When you're mindful of your energy, you'll handle situations differently and protect yourself in ways that allow you to stay aligned with your goals. Your energy is sacred, and protecting it is an essential part of your self-care and self-development. Don't waste it—empower yourself by recognizing what lifts you up and what brings you down.

takers: | givers:

BUILD YOUR AFFIRMATIONS

"A belief is just a thought you keep thinking." —
Abraham Hicks

The problem is that the more you continuously think
about something, the more you will find evidence for it,
and soon you'll believe it to be true—whether it's good
or bad. This repetition is what also programs your
subconscious mind.

But don't worry—just as you've programmed your
current belief system, you can reprogram it so that it
actually supports and serves you.

We do that with affirmations. For affirmations to work,
they need to directly replace your limiting beliefs. For
example, let's say you believe that only bad people
have a lot of money. An affirmation like "Money flows
to me easily and effortlessly" probably won't work.
Why? Because that would imply that you are a bad
person, and since I highly doubt that you are—and
your subconscious mind knows that too—you would
subconsciously sabotage that affirmation to avoid
receiving money.
Why? Because you don't want to be seen as a bad
person. Does that make sense?

We need to tackle your limiting belief and find a way to
prove it wrong! Start by finding evidence—look for
people online or in your life who are wealthy and also
good people. Then, create an affirmation like, "I can do
so much good with the money that flows to me" or "I
can support so many businesses with the money I
receive." Do you see where this is going?

"On the left side, I want you to write down all the limiting beliefs that feel icky, and then work to turn them into positive affirmations that support your growth.

Use these affirmations as a tool to reprogram your mind. You'll want to read, speak out loud, and repeat your affirmations first thing in the morning and right before you go to bed at night.

I once worked with an energy healer who recommended repeating affirmations 40 times a day. So let's get serious! Have fun with it—you can literally program your subconscious mind.
Isn't that exciting?

limiting belief: affirmation:

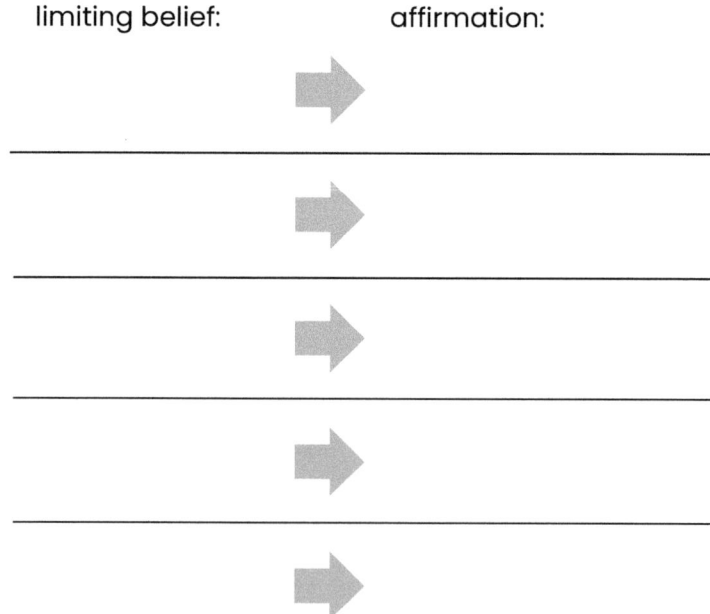

BUILD YOUR AFFIRMATIONS:

limiting belief: affirmation:

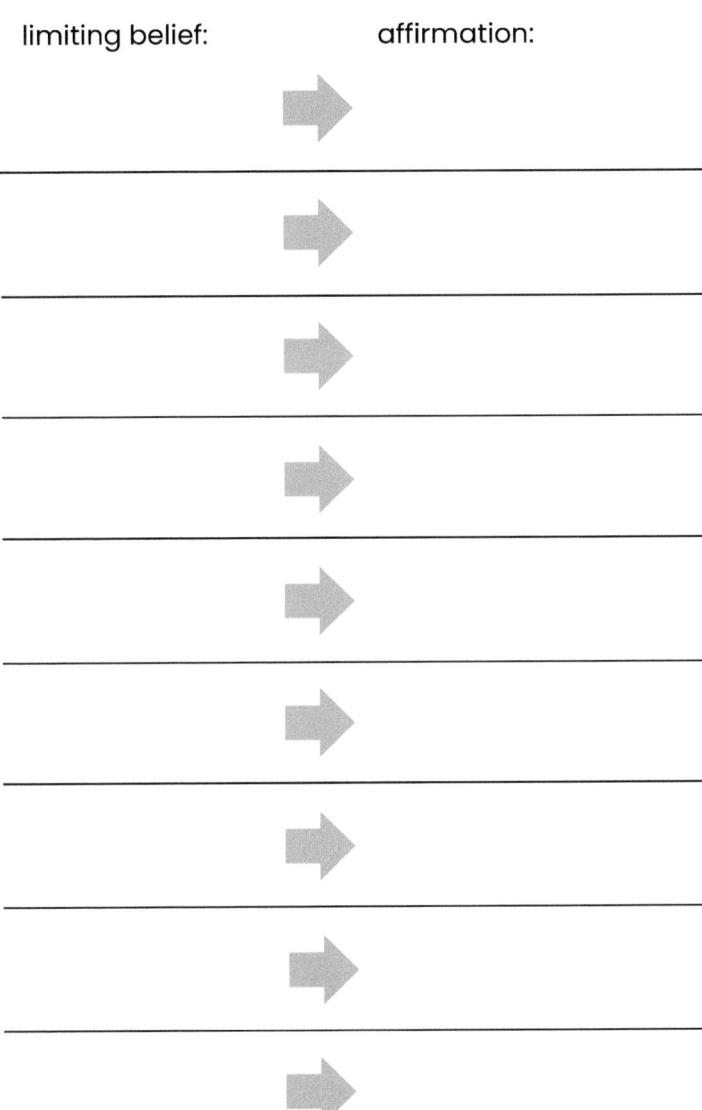

limiting belief: affirmation:

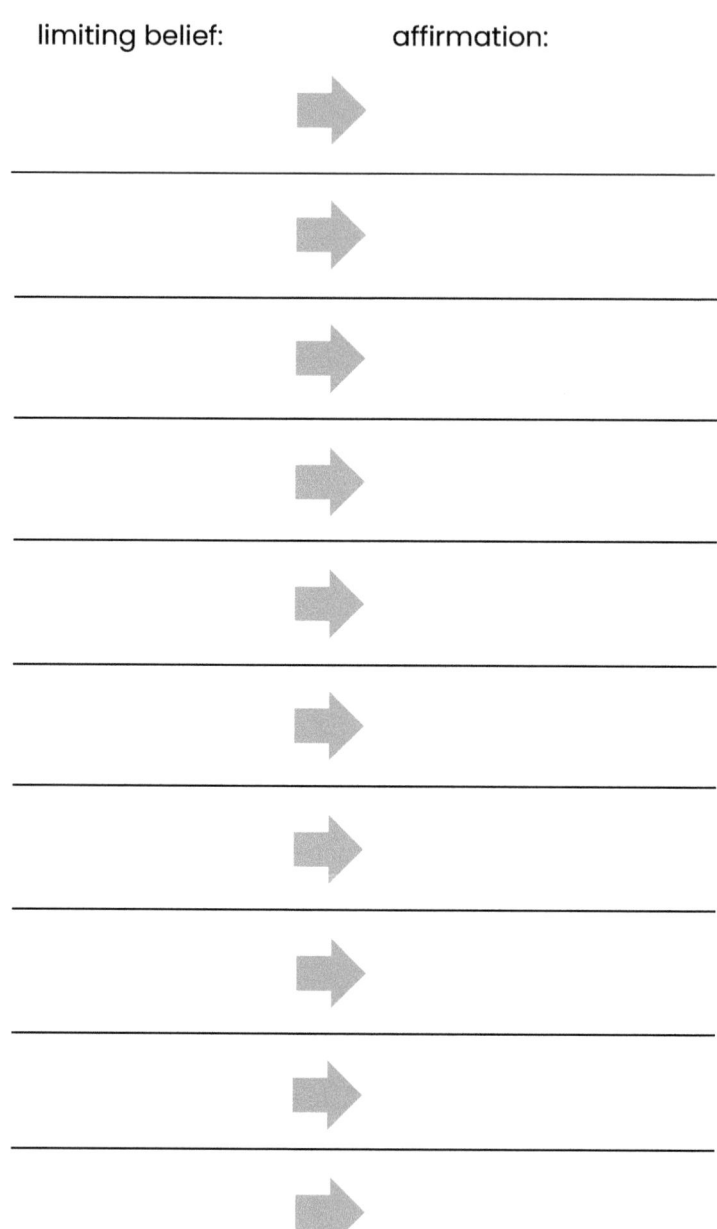

GAIN CLARITY

I love this exercise so much!

It's not until you actually reflect on how you've been approaching things that you start to see how they seem to spiral by themselves (which isn't true, by the way). Only then can you begin to turn things around and make real changes.

This is exactly what we're doing right now.

You know how when you do one thing, it leads to another? That's what we're writing down right now—so you can become aware of your patterns and behaviors and understand how they affect your journey through this 6-month transformation.

Be fully honest with yourself! You're only holding yourself back when you try to "smooth things out." Here's where the magic happens: once you've recognized your patterns, it becomes much easier to create a game plan that serves you. These new, positive patterns and behaviors will move you toward your goals and start building momentum.

Over the next 6 months, you'll notice how everything begins to align with your intentions for growth. That's exactly the transformation we're aiming for!
So, let's get really real on the left side, then come up with action steps on the right side that will empower you and guide you toward becoming your best self.

old way: new way:

thoughts

decisions

actions

experience

"old" you   "new" you

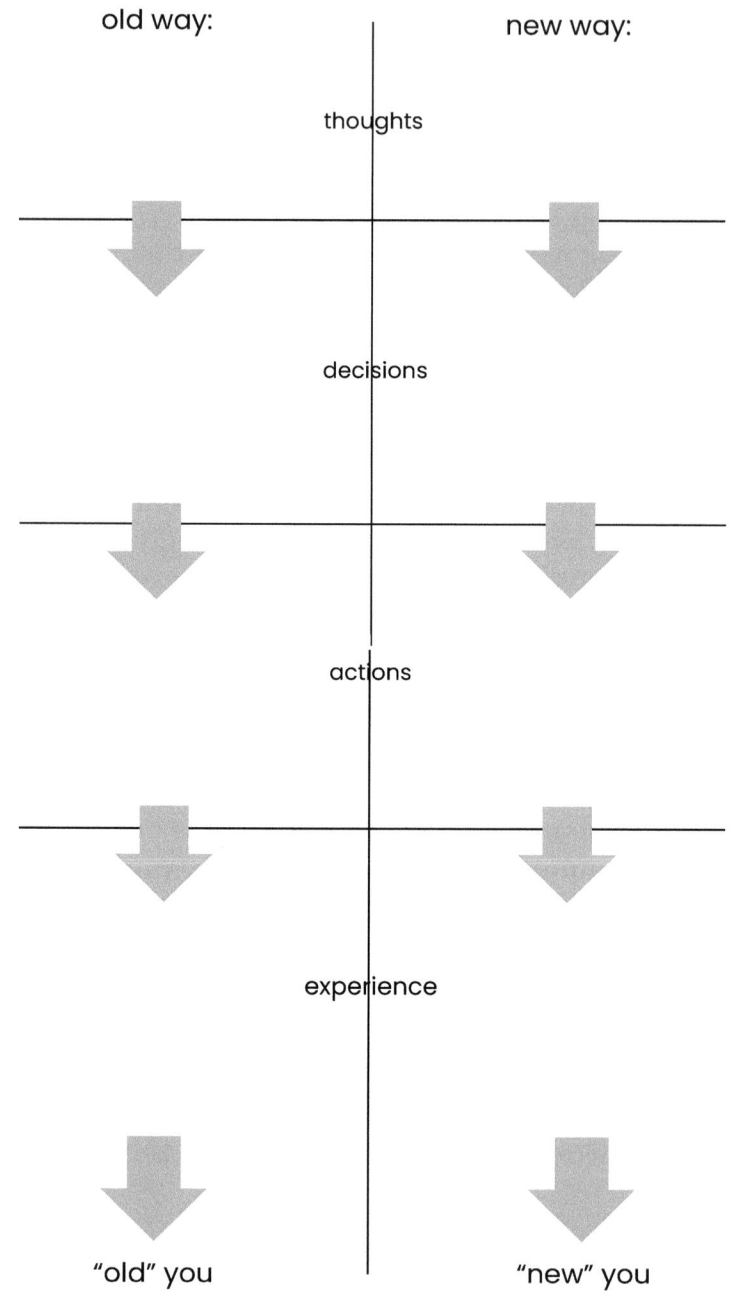

THE TRANSFORMATION GAME PLAN

I'm not sure if you fully realize it, but the amount of work you've already invested in yourself—how much you've reflected on your thoughts, beliefs, actions, and patterns—is intense, in the most beautiful way.

I understand that you've probably had a lot of painful moments, maybe even tears. For sure, you've had many eye-opening, Oprah-style "AHA" moments, and probably some cringe-worthy moments too. Let's be honest—who really wants to face and work through their own mess?! But you know it's necessary to come out stronger, wiser, and better on the other side.

This kind of self-help and personal development will serve you for the rest of your life! No matter how long it took to get here, no matter how many interruptions, or how many times you felt like tossing this journal aside because it hurts to dig deep—you made it! That's something to be especially proud of. I am so proud of you!

Now we're getting to the good part—the "fasten your seatbelt, we're taking off" part. We're getting down to business.

I need you to remember the intention you set earlier, along with the goals you established for these 6 months. Do you remember? Having goals is great, but they don't mean much if you don't know how to realize and achieve them, right? A goal without a plan is just a dream. It's like "wishing on a star." Not in this journal. We dream—and then we achieve.

This practice will guide you to create a game plan! It will lead you from what you're aiming for to the single steps you need to take to get there. Trust the process and follow the prompts. Trust your intuition—usually, the first thought you have when reading a prompt is what you need to write down. Don't overthink it. Just trust it, no matter how bold or over the top it seems.

By the way, remember how I encouraged you to focus on growth and expansion? Well, I want to remind you that empowerment comes from taking charge of your goals and staying aligned with your intentions. If your goals or priorities feel misaligned, don't hesitate to adjust them. Change is normal and should be expected over the course of 6 months—I welcome it! It means we're progressing and doing something right. Did I mention how proud I am of you?

That's why these exercises are designed to be repeated whenever you feel things are no longer aligned.

Let's start!

> *Move in silence!*
> ## WE LET RESULTS DO THE TALKING.

YOUR SELF-WORTH

The truth to finally becoming your best self is deceptively simple—and yet so challenging to implement. At the end of the day, it all comes down to your self-worth. Why?

When you visualize your dreams and desires, they stem from the version of you who knows you're worthy of all that and more. However, if you're not experiencing those visions in your life right now, it's because past circumstances and decisions have led you to the place where you currently feel stuck. Correct me if I'm wrong, but if you had made those decisions from the version of yourself who fully understood her worth, you wouldn't be in this position. You wouldn't have tolerated behavior from others or accepted circumstances that didn't align with what truly feels right for you. Right?
This journal, along with all the practices it contains, is designed to guide and support you in understanding your self-worth—and, more importantly, in standing firmly in that power.

To help you embrace your self-worth and step into your most empowered self, visit
WWW.KATHRINELOUIS.COM/MEDITATIONS
for guided meditations. Even if you've never meditated before, these sessions are perfect for winding down and reconnecting with your true self.

TRANSFORMATION GAME PLAN:

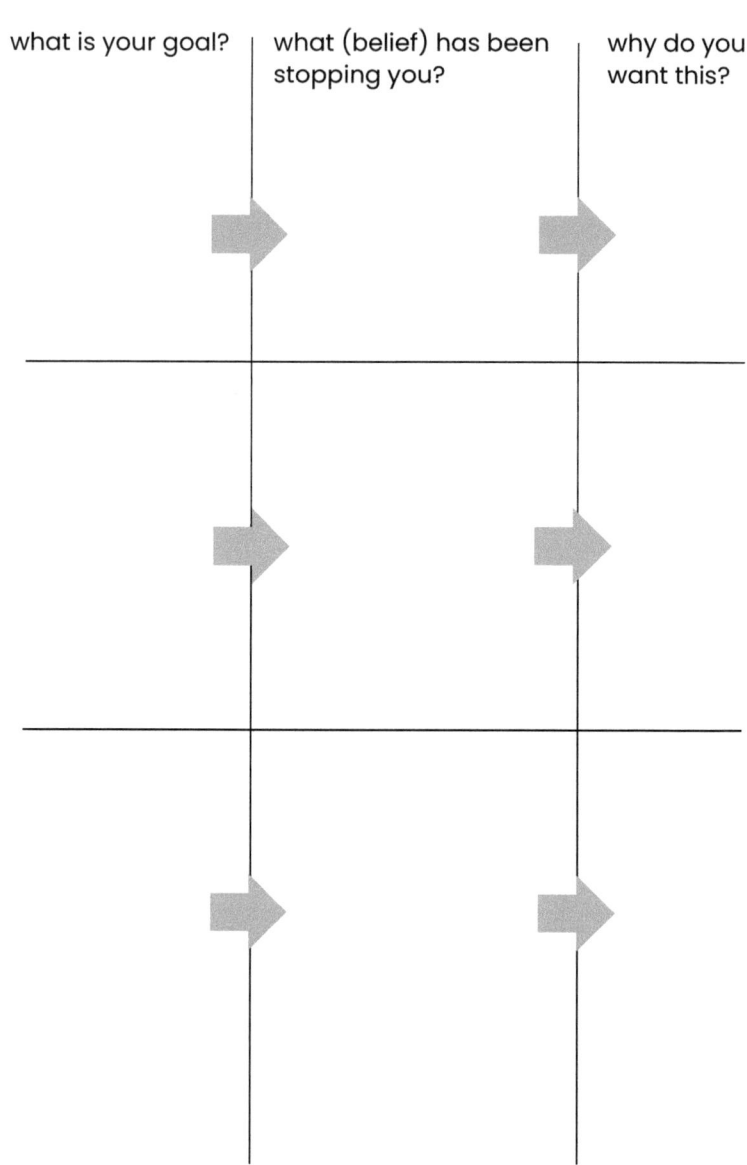

what is your goal?

what (belief) has been stopping you?

why do you want this?

what would your
best/ highest self,
"her" do?

the actions you will
take to achieve this
goal:

new habit(s)
that will support
the process:

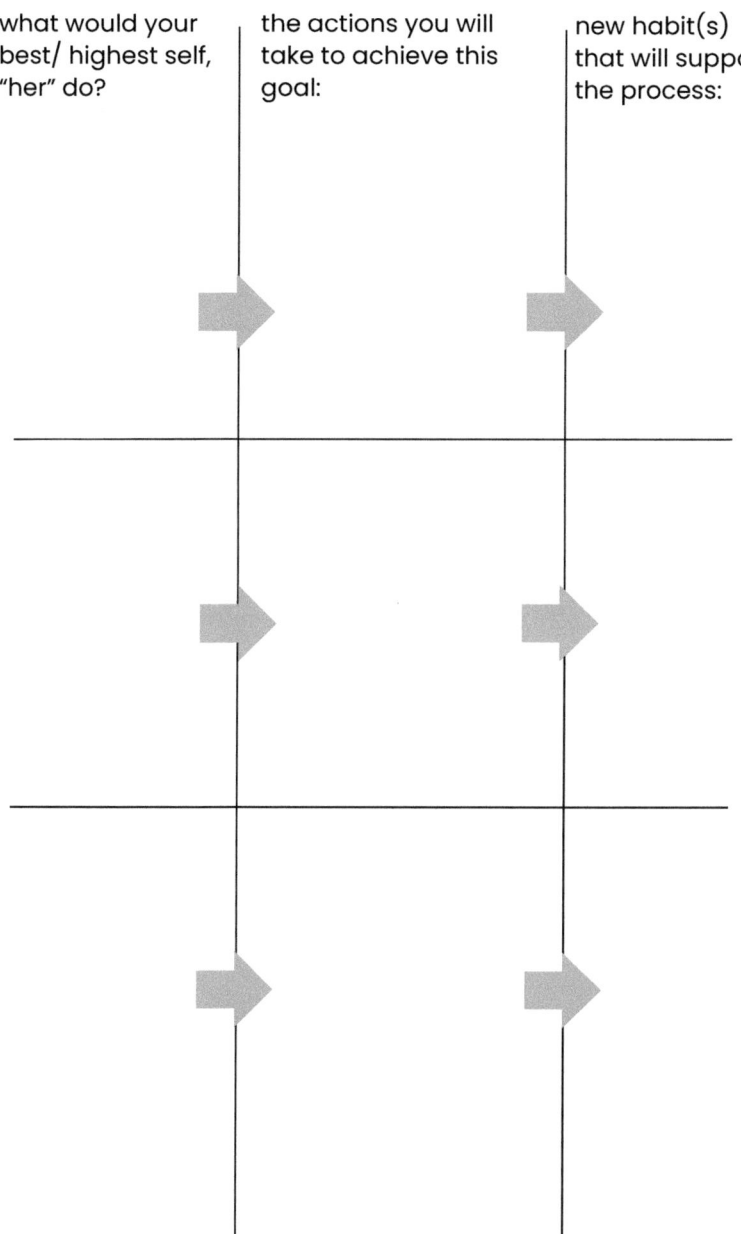

HOW & WHY TO BUILD YOUR SELF CARE COLLECTION

You might wonder: What is a Self-Care Collection?
A Self-Care Collection is a personal list where you save all your favorite self-care routines—those things that make you feel nothing less than amazing!

Why is this so important? Especially when times get rough, and you're feeling stressed or even burned out, your brain often doesn't have the capacity to remember those moments of self-care that bring you peace. That's exactly why we're creating this collection now—so that during your 6-month transformation journey, whenever you feel overwhelmed, you can easily refer back to this list and choose something you know will soothe your soul in that very moment.

Nurturing yourself when you need it the most, and paying attention to what you truly deserve, will not only help you get back into alignment faster but will also boost your self-worth. Taking care of yourself is a habit that can be learned, and it's a key part of your personal empowerment. You absolutely deserve that!

A self-care routine can be anything that feels soothing to your soul—something that helps you relax and feel at peace. It might be meditating, taking a bubble bath with candles, creating art, visiting a museum, or even going on a motorcycle ride.

Enjoy the process, let your mind wander, and remember—you deserve to feel empowered, rejuvenated, and at peace!

BUILD YOUR OWN SELF CARE COLLECTION

collect your most favorite self-care moments right here and
come back often for inspiration!

....

....

....

....

....

....

....

....

....

....

....

....

....

....

....

....

....

....

MONTH 1

SET YOUR TOP 3 GOALS FOR OUR FIRST MONTH:

Let's get serious and start with our very first month! HOW exciting! I am so excited for you and cannot wait to see the incredible progress you're about to make.

When choosing your top 3 goals for each month, it's important to stay aligned with the main goals you set at the beginning of this journey. Think about what truly matters to you—whether it's growing your business, strengthening your well-being, or achieving personal milestones. Your goals should reflect the vision you've created for the next 6 months. This is how you'll continue to grow in the areas that are most important to you.

I know it can be easy to get lost when setting goals. Sometimes we set too many, or we get distracted and focus on goals that don't align with what we actually want. But here's the secret: clarity is the key to your success. By focusing on just three goals per month, you're giving yourself the power to make real progress without overwhelming yourself. Each small win builds the momentum you need to achieve big things.

So let's focus on the goals that light you up—the ones that move you toward the empowered and successful version of yourself that you've always wanted to be. Go back to your Transformation Game Plan and trust the path you're on. You've already laid the foundation—now it's time to take action and watch your life transform.

This is your moment. You've made the decision to show up for yourself and create the life you truly desire. Remember, you have the strength, the clarity, and the power to make it happen.

You are capable of achieving so much more than you even realize. This isn't just about setting goals—this is about becoming the person you've always dreamed of being.

You deserve to live a life of abundance, joy, and purpose. You deserve to become your most empowered and successful self—and the journey starts right here.
Let's start!

THE MOVE YOU'RE
SCARED TO MAKE
COULD BE THE ONE
changing your life.

YOUR 3 GOALS FOR THIS MONTH

(in alignment with your main goals):

goal:

the action(s) you will
take to achieve them:

1.

2.

3.

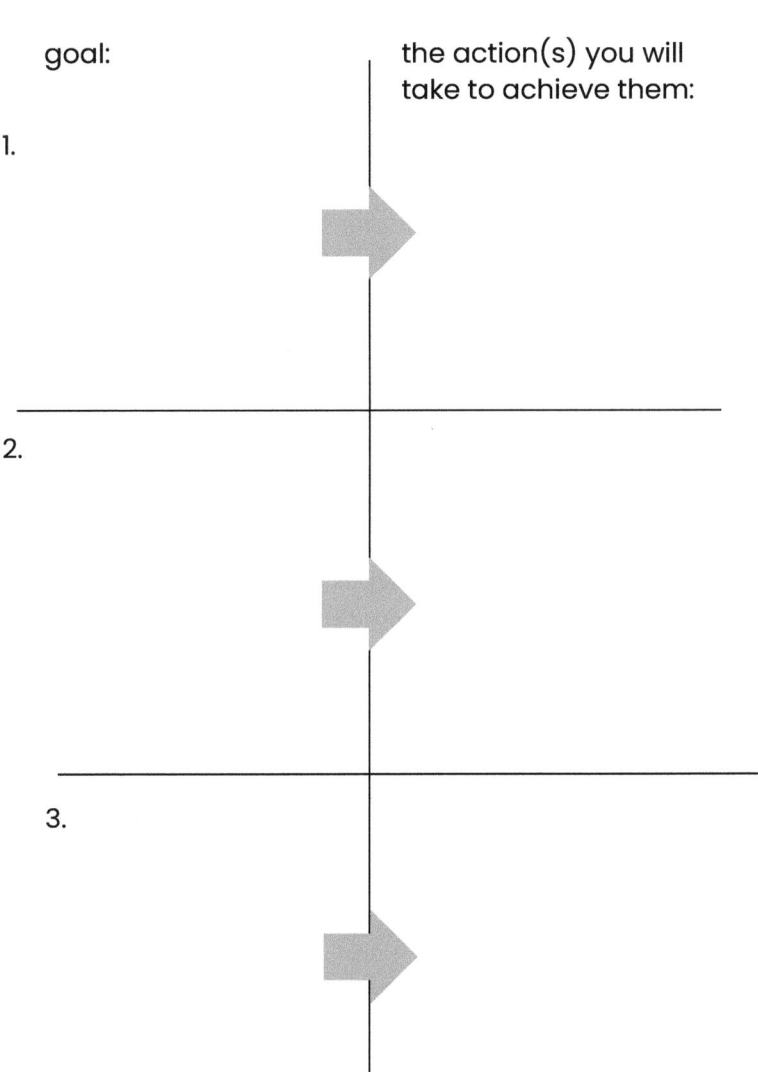

SET YOUR GOALS FOR THIS WEEK

Let's start with our very first week—whooohooo! I'm literally sitting here cheerleading for you, and I couldn't be more excited! This is the beginning of something incredible, and I'm so proud of you for showing up for yourself.

Remember, this is your chance to reinvent yourself, to become the person you've always dreamed of being. With the tools in this 6-month transformation journal, you're not just setting goals—you're creating the life you've always wanted. You've already taken the first step, and now it's time to take action and make it real.

So, what were the three main goals you set for this month? Now, let's focus on turning those big goals into achievable actions. Break them down into steps you can take this week. Think about what's manageable but still bold, and assign each step to the life areas they belong to. What are the first, most important steps you can take this week? That's where your focus goes!

You don't need to fill in every life area—just focus on the ones that align with your priorities. And here's a powerful truth: you don't need to have the entire path figured out right now. You just need to take the next right step. When you stay focused on your goals and move step by step, the rest will unfold in ways that will surprise and empower you.

This is the moment where transformation happens, where you turn dreams into reality—one action at a time.

Every step you take is bringing you closer to the empowered and successful version of yourself that you were always meant to be. This journey is yours, and you're more than capable of achieving everything you set your mind to.

Trust yourself, trust the process, and get ready to see just how powerful you are. You've got this!

self care & wellness	career & business
finance	family & friends
physical environment	self development

DAILY JOURNALING - WEEK 1

This kind of daily journaling changed my life!
And yes, I know that sounds dramatic—like those are
big words—but it's completely true!

This kind of daily journaling will allow you to stay
focused, to keep your eye on the prize, and the impact
it will have on your life is immeasurable. The best part?
It only takes a couple of minutes each day—and you'll
enjoy it so much that it'll become a daily habit you
look forward to.

This is the only kind of journaling I never had to
convince myself to do. Why? Because the results are
so powerful. The way you'll quickly start to feel the shift
in your life and experience real change will have you
loving this journaling process in no time.
And hey, if you ever get interrupted or miss a few days,
don't worry! Just jump right back in. You'll feel the relief
of being focused again soon enough.

One of my favorite things about this type of journaling
is being able to naturally track the results. Focusing on
three key things each day might not seem like much,
but over time, the way it accumulates is massive.

Remember, it's much better to focus on just three key
priorities each day than to try to do everything and
end up feeling overwhelmed. In the long run, this
approach will take you so much further—and you'll get
there faster, too. You'll start to notice that you're more
effective, more productive, and even more relaxed.
Why? Because you're getting things done without the
stress and overwhelm.

You'll feel more organized, more in control, and you'll start to see how your life begins to shift as you stick with this technique.
Just trust the process and watch how things begin to unfold. You've got this!

IDEAS ARE POWER.
EXECUTION IS MAGIC.
Make it happen.

week: | your intention for this week:

YOUR TOP 3 PRIORITIES TODAY:

	mon	tues	wed
1.			
2.			
3.			

YOUR BLESSINGS TODAY:

♡ ☐ ☐ ☐   ♡ ☐ ☐ ☐   ♡ ☐ ☐ ☐
☐ ☐ ☐   ☐ ☐ ☐   ☐ ☐ ☐
☐ ☐ ☐   ☐ ☐ ☐   ☐ ☐ ☐

what will you no longer hold on to this week?

	thur	fri	sat/ sun
1.			
2.			
3.			

YOUR BLESSINGS TODAY:

YOUR INNER GPS
CONNECTING TO YOUR INTUITION

Your intuition is your inner GPS. And I mean it.

Just like the GPS in your car, where you type in the destination you want to reach—your desires are your personal destinations, and your intuition is always guiding you there. The magic happens when you truly listen to that inner voice. Those nudges, those little pulls, that sense of knowing out of nowhere—no matter how crazy or unexpected it feels—are all part of your inner wisdom speaking to you.

And let's be honest, we've all had moments where, in hindsight, we thought, "If only I had followed that idea" or "Why didn't I trust my gut?" But here's the truth: your intuition is always on your side, and you can start making it a powerful, natural part of your life right now. To do that, it's important to strengthen that connection —ideally on a daily basis. I had a client once start by choosing her morning coffee cup using only her intuition! With you, I have something even more powerful in mind. It's all about tuning into yourself and building that trust.

Here's what I want you to do: take a moment of stillness. Place your right hand on your belly, your left hand on your heart. Now ask your intuition, "How can I achieve XYZ (insert your goal)?" Stay in this stillness as long as it feels good. Some call it meditating, others call it focusing—whatever you call it, embrace the quiet.

Your answer may come instantly, or it might reveal

itself within the next 24 hours. Sometimes, you're being guided by the choices you make afterward without even realizing it. So pay attention to the small signs and signals around you—they matter!

Write down everything you feel or receive after asking the question. Putting it on paper will help you recognize just how much guidance you're already receiving. You'll be amazed at how powerful your intuition really is when you start listening.

Trust yourself, because every answer you seek is already within you. When you honor your inner voice, you unlock the power to create anything you desire. You've got this!

....

....

....

....

....

....

....

....

....

YOUR INNER GPS
CONNECTING TO YOUR INTUITION

....

....

....

....

....

....

....

....

....

....

....

....

....

....

....

....

To strengthen your relationship with your intuition—
your inner GPS—come back to this practice as often as
possible, ideally daily. Bookmark these pages, and let
your intuition guide you every step of the way as you
move toward your dreams.

YOUR WEEKLY REFLECTION

CONGRATULATIONS! You made it through your first week— how did it go?

Take a moment to celebrate yourself—you've just taken a massive step forward! What were your first accomplishments? What insights did you gain? What did you learn about yourself?

Use these pages to explore how you did with your weekly goals. Reflect on what worked, what felt aligned, and where you may have needed to adjust or pivot. There's no right or wrong here—this is about progress, self-awareness, and learning what drives you forward.

Did you achieve your goals this week? Did you need to shift your actions? Write down every thought, insight, and feeling. This is your space for self-discovery and growth—a chance to connect with yourself on a deeper level and see how much you're evolving. And don't worry if you need more space—there are additional pages at the end of the journal for more free-flowing journaling.

These reflection pages are a powerful tool designed to help you stay aligned and focused throughout the next 6 months. This is YOUR time to learn, to grow, and to become the person you've always dreamed of being. You have everything you need within you to make this journey a success.

Keep going—you are unstoppable, and the best is yet to come!

WEEKLY REFLECTION:

self care & wellness	career & business
finance	family & friends
physical environment	self development

....

....

....

....

....

....

....

WEEKLY REFLECTION:

....

....

....

....

....

....

....

....

....

....

....

....

....

....

....

....

....

....

YOUR GOALS FOR THIS WEEK:

make sure to double check to stay in alignment
with monthly goals

self care & wellness	career & business
finance	family & friends
physical environment	self development

....

....

....

....

....

....

....

....

....

....

....

....

....

....

....

....

....

....

....

....

....

....

....

....

....

....

YOUR TOP 3 PRIORITIES TODAY:

mon	tues	wed

1.

2.

3.

YOUR BLESSINGS TODAY:

♡ ☐ ☐ ☐   ♡ ☐ ☐ ☐   ♡ ☐ ☐ ☐

☐ ☐ ☐   ☐ ☐ ☐   ☐ ☐ ☐

☐ ☐ ☐   ☐ ☐ ☐   ☐ ☐ ☐

what will you no longer hold on to this week?

	thur	fri	sat/ sun
1.			
2.			
3.			

YOUR BLESSINGS TODAY:

YOUR INNER GPS
CONNECTING TO YOUR INTUITION

YOUR INNER GPS
CONNECTING TO YOUR INTUITION

....

....

....

....

....

....

....

....

....

....

....

....

....

....

....

....

....

....

WEEKLY REFLECTION:

self care & wellness	career & business
finance	**family & friends**
physical environment	**self development**

....

....

....

....

....

....

....

YOUR GOALS FOR THIS WEEK:

make sure to double check to stay in alignment
with monthly goals

self care & wellness	career & business
finance	family & friends
physical environment	self development

....

....

....

....

....

....

week: | your intention for this week:

YOUR TOP 3 PRIORITIES TODAY:

	mon	tues	wed
1.			
2.			
3.			

YOUR BLESSINGS TODAY:

what will you no longer hold on to this week?

	thur	fri	sat/ sun
1.			
2.			
3.			

YOUR BLESSINGS TODAY:

♡ ☐ ☐ ☐   ♡ ☐ ☐ ☐   ♡ ☐ ☐ ☐
☐ ☐ ☐   ☐ ☐ ☐   ☐ ☐ ☐
☐ ☐ ☐   ☐ ☐ ☐   ☐ ☐ ☐

YOUR INNER GPS
CONNECTING TO YOUR INTUITION

YOUR INNER GPS
CONNECTING TO YOUR INTUITION

....
....
....
....
....
....
....
....
....
....
....
....
....
....
....
....
....
....

WEEKLY REFLECTION:

self care & wellness	career & business
finance	family & friends
physical environment	self development

....
....
....
....
....
....
....

YOUR GOALS FOR THIS WEEK:

make sure to double check to stay in alignment
with monthly goals

self care & wellness	career & business
finance	family & friends
physical environment	self development

....

....

....

....

....

....

YOUR TOP 3 PRIORITIES TODAY:

mon	tues	wed

1.

2.

3.

YOUR BLESSINGS TODAY:

♡ ☐ ☐ ☐   ♡ ☐ ☐ ☐   ♡ ☐ ☐ ☐
☐ ☐ ☐   ☐ ☐ ☐   ☐ ☐ ☐
☐ ☐ ☐   ☐ ☐ ☐   ☐ ☐ ☐

what will you no longer hold on to this week?

	thur	fri	sat/ sun
1.			
2.			
3.			

YOUR BLESSINGS TODAY:

♡ ☐ ☐ ☐   ♡ ☐ ☐ ☐   ♡ ☐ ☐ ☐
☐ ☐ ☐   ☐ ☐ ☐   ☐ ☐ ☐
☐ ☐ ☐   ☐ ☐ ☐   ☐ ☐ ☐

YOUR INNER GPS
CONNECTING TO YOUR INTUITION

YOUR INNER GPS
CONNECTING TO YOUR INTUITION

....

....

....

....

....

....

....

....

....

....

....

....

....

....

....

....

....

....

....

WEEKLY REFLECTION:

self care & wellness	career & business
finance	family & friends
physical environment	self development

....
....
....
....
....
....
....

MONTHLY REFLECTION

WOW! You've just completed the first month of your 6-month transformation journey, and that is a huge achievement!
You've shown up for yourself, embraced new habits, and taken the first powerful steps toward creating lasting change. This is only the beginning, and there's so much more growth and success ahead.

On the following pages, I invite you to reflect on this first month. What goals did you set at the start? How have you begun to shift and grow in these early stages? What have you learned about yourself? Celebrate every small win and recognize how far you've already come on your path to personal transformation.

This month wasn't just about checking off tasks—it was about laying the foundation for your self-development and success. The habits you've started to build and the insights you've gained are planting the seeds for your future success.

And guess what? This is just the start! The journey ahead is filled with even more opportunities for personal growth, self-discovery, and confidence building. As you move into the next month, keep building on your momentum. Stay committed to your journaling practice, your reflections, and your goals.

You are limitless, and the more you keep showing up for yourself, the more you'll realize how much you're truly capable of. Keep going—you've only just scratched the surface of what's possible!

MONTHLY REFLECTION:

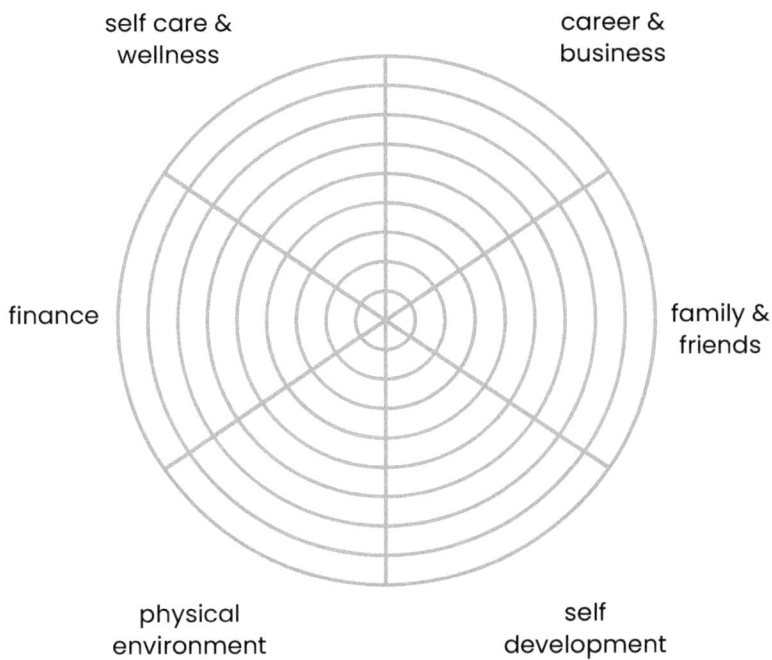

self care &
wellness

career &
business

finance

family &
friends

physical
environment

self
development

Just like with your first inventory wheel, the following
pages give you space to go deeper into each area of
your life. Be honest and open—the more honest you
are, the more clarity and growth you'll experience.

self care & wellness

....

....

....

....

....

....

career & business

....

....

....

....

....

....

finance

....

....

....

....

....

family & friends

....

....

....

....

....

....

physical environment

....

....

....

....

....

....

self development

....

....

....

....

....

....

....

....

....

....

....

....

....

....

....

....

....

....

....

MONTHLY GOALS PROCESS BAR

how far did I come so far? track your progress right
here
(and don´t forget to be proud of yourself!) :

ADDITIONAL JOURNALING

MONTH 2

YOU CAN.
AND YOU WILL.

*period.

**also the name of my podcast by no coincidence.

YOUR 3 GOALS FOR THIS MONTH

(in alignment with your main goals):

goal:

the action(s) you will
take to achieve them:

1.

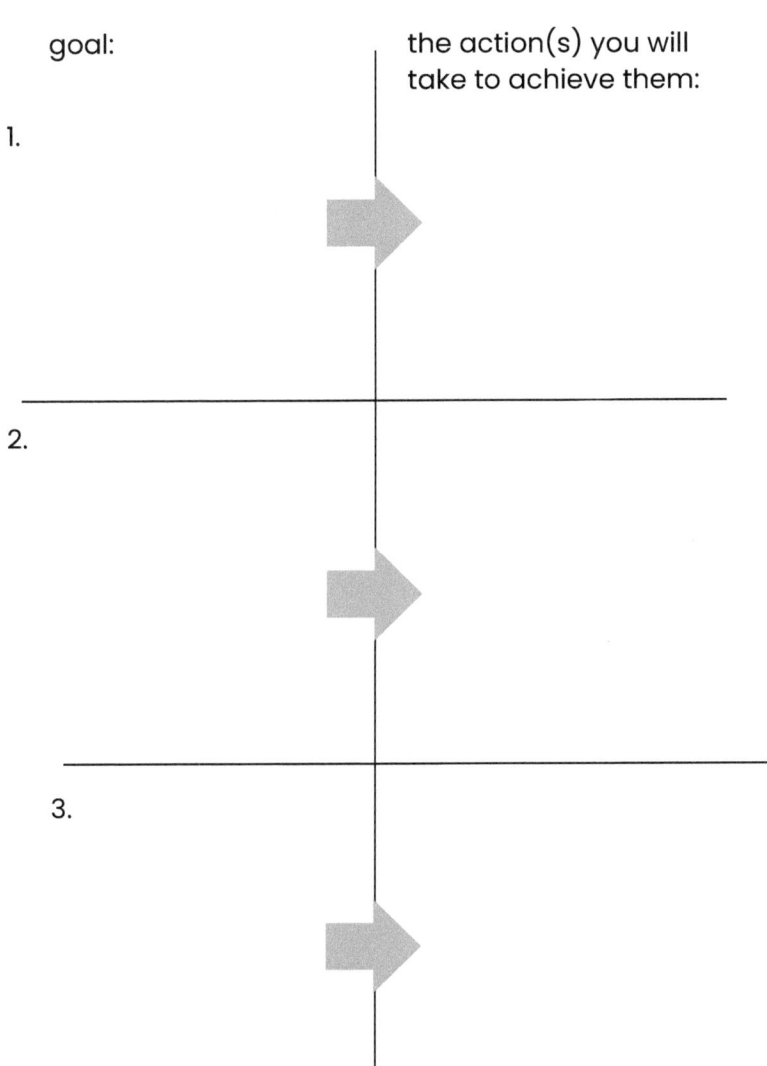

2.

3.

YOUR GOALS FOR THIS WEEK:

make sure to double check to stay in alignment
with monthly goals

self care & wellness	career & business
finance	family & friends
physical environment	self development

....

....

....

....

....

....

YOUR INNER GPS
CONNECTING TO YOUR INTUITION

YOUR INNER GPS
CONNECTING TO YOUR INTUITION

....

....

....

....

....

....

....

....

....

....

....

....

....

....

....

....

WEEKLY REFLECTION:

self care & wellness	career & business
finance	family & friends
physical environment	self development

....
....
....
....
....
....
....

....

....

....

....

....

....

....

....

....

....

....

....

....

....

....

....

....

....

....

....

YOUR GOALS FOR THIS WEEK:

make sure to double check to stay in alignment
with monthly goals

self care & wellness	career & business
finance	family & friends
physical environment	self development

....

....

....

....

....

....

week: | your intention for this week:

YOUR TOP 3 PRIORITIES TODAY:

	mon	tues	wed
1.			
2.			
3.			

YOUR BLESSINGS TODAY:

♡ ☐ ☐ ☐   ♡ ☐ ☐ ☐   ♡ ☐ ☐ ☐
☐ ☐ ☐   ☐ ☐ ☐   ☐ ☐ ☐
☐ ☐ ☐   ☐ ☐ ☐   ☐ ☐ ☐

what will you no longer hold on to this week?

	thur	fri	sat/ sun
1.			
2.			
3.			

YOUR BLESSINGS TODAY:

YOUR INNER GPS
CONNECTING TO YOUR INTUITION

YOUR INNER GPS
CONNECTING TO YOUR INTUITION

....

....

....

....

....

....

....

....

....

....

....

....

....

....

....

....

....

....

WEEKLY REFLECTION:

self care & wellness	career & business
finance	family & friends
physical environment	self development

YOUR GOALS FOR THIS WEEK:

make sure to double check to stay in alignment
with monthly goals

self care & wellness	career & business
finance	family & friends
physical environment	self development

....

....

....

....

....

....

| week: | your intention for this week: |

YOUR TOP 3 PRIORITIES TODAY:

mon	tues	wed

1.

2.

3.

YOUR BLESSINGS TODAY:

♡ ☐ ☐ ☐   ♡ ☐ ☐ ☐   ♡ ☐ ☐ ☐
☐ ☐ ☐   ☐ ☐ ☐   ☐ ☐ ☐
☐ ☐ ☐   ☐ ☐ ☐   ☐ ☐ ☐

what will you no longer hold on to this week?

	thur	fri	sat/ sun
1.			
2.			
3.			

YOUR BLESSINGS TODAY:

YOUR INNER GPS
CONNECTING TO YOUR INTUITION

YOUR INNER GPS
CONNECTING TO YOUR INTUITION

....
....
....
....
....
....
....
....
....
....
....
....
....
....
....
....
....
....

WEEKLY REFLECTION:

self care & wellness	career & business
finance	family & friends
physical environment	self development

....

....

....

....

....

....

....

YOUR GOALS FOR THIS WEEK:

make sure to double check to stay in alignment
with monthly goals

self care & wellness	career & business
finance	family & friends
physical environment	self development

....

....

....

....

....

....

week:

your intention for this week:

YOUR TOP 3 PRIORITIES TODAY:

	mon	tues	wed
1.			
2.			
3.			

YOUR BLESSINGS TODAY:

♡ ☐ ☐ ☐   ♡ ☐ ☐ ☐   ♡ ☐ ☐ ☐
☐ ☐ ☐   ☐ ☐ ☐   ☐ ☐ ☐
☐ ☐ ☐   ☐ ☐ ☐   ☐ ☐ ☐

what will you no longer hold on to this week?

	thur	fri	sat/ sun
1.			
2.			
3.			

YOUR BLESSINGS TODAY:

YOUR INNER GPS
CONNECTING TO YOUR INTUITION

YOUR INNER GPS
CONNECTING TO YOUR INTUITION

....

....

....

....

....

....

....

....

....

....

....

....

....

....

....

....

....

....

....

....

....

WEEKLY REFLECTION:

self care & wellness	career & business
finance	family & friends
physical environment	self development

....

....

....

....

....

....

MONTHLY REFLECTION

WOW! You've just completed the first month of your 6-month transformation journey, and that is a huge achievement!
You've shown up for yourself, embraced new habits, and taken the first powerful steps toward creating lasting change. This is only the beginning, and there's so much more growth and success ahead.

On the following pages, I invite you to reflect on this first month. What goals did you set at the start? How have you begun to shift and grow in these early stages? What have you learned about yourself? Celebrate every small win and recognize how far you've already come on your path to personal transformation.

This month wasn't just about checking off tasks—it was about laying the foundation for your self-development and success. The habits you've started to build and the insights you've gained are planting the seeds for your future success.

And guess what? This is just the start! The journey ahead is filled with even more opportunities for personal growth, self-discovery, and confidence building. As you move into the next month, keep building on your momentum. Stay committed to your journaling practice, your reflections, and your goals.

You are limitless, and the more you keep showing up for yourself, the more you'll realize how much you're truly capable of. Keep going—you've only just scratched the surface of what's possible!

MONTHLY REFLECTION:

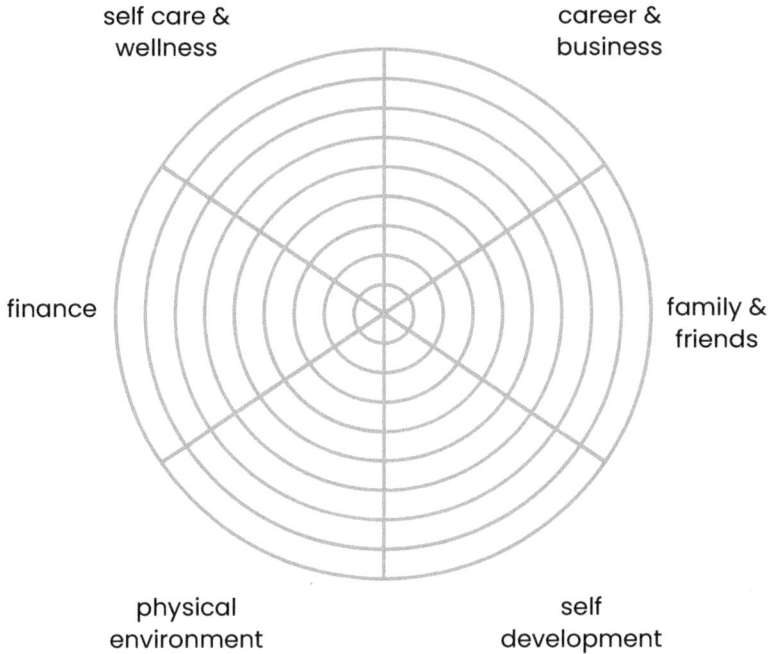

self care &
wellness

career &
business

finance

family &
friends

physical
environment

self
development

Just like with your first inventory wheel, the following
pages give you space to go deeper into each area of
your life. Be honest and open—the more honest you
are, the more clarity and growth you'll experience.

self care & wellness

....

....

....

....

....

....

career & business

....

....

....

....

....

....

finance

....

....

....

....

....

family & friends

....

....

....

....

....

....

physical environment

....

....

....

....

....

....

self development

....

....

....

....

....

....

....

....

....

....

....

....

....

....

....

....

....

....

....

MONTHLY GOALS PROCESS BAR

how far did I come so far? track your progress right
here
(and don´t forget to be proud of yourself!) :

○────────────────○────────────────○

ADDITIONAL JOURNALING

MONTH 3

THE MORE YOU KNOW YOURSELF, THE MORE CLARITY THERE IS

on your path.

YOUR 3 GOALS FOR THIS MONTH

(in alignment with your main goals):

goal:

the action(s) you will
take to achieve them:

1.

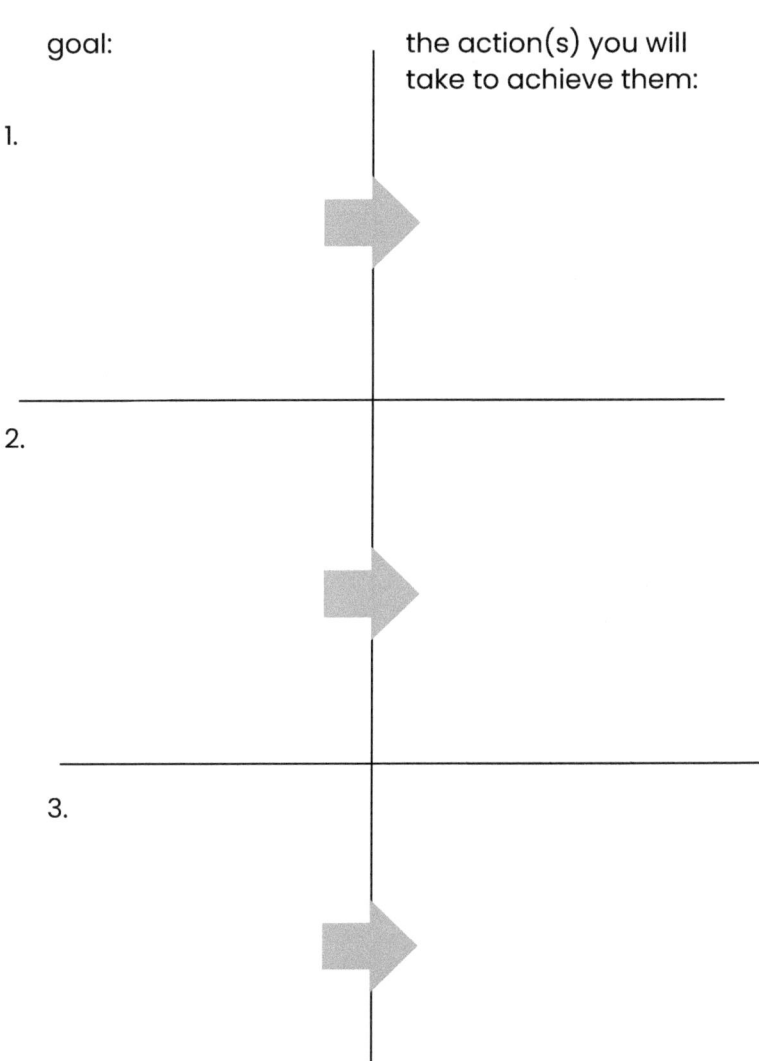

2.

3.

YOUR GOALS FOR THIS WEEK:

make sure to double check to stay in alignment
with monthly goals

self care & wellness	career & business
finance	family & friends
physical environment	self development

....

....

....

....

....

....

YOUR INNER GPS
CONNECTING TO YOUR INTUITION

YOUR INNER GPS
CONNECTING TO YOUR INTUITION

....

....

....

....

....

....

....

....

....

....

....

....

....

....

....

....

....

....

....

WEEKLY REFLECTION:

self care & wellness	career & business
finance	family & friends
physical environment	self development

YOUR GOALS FOR THIS WEEK:

make sure to double check to stay in alignment
with monthly goals

self care & wellness	career & business
finance	family & friends
physical environment	self development

....

....

....

....

....

....

week: ☐ your intention for this week:

YOUR TOP 3 PRIORITIES TODAY:

	mon	tues	wed
1.			
2.			
3.			

YOUR BLESSINGS TODAY:

what will you no longer hold on to this week?

	thur	fri	sat/ sun
1.			
2.			
3.			

YOUR BLESSINGS TODAY:

♡ ☐ ☐ ☐   ♡ ☐ ☐ ☐   ♡ ☐ ☐ ☐
☐ ☐ ☐   ☐ ☐ ☐   ☐ ☐ ☐
☐ ☐ ☐   ☐ ☐ ☐   ☐ ☐ ☐

YOUR INNER GPS
CONNECTING TO YOUR INTUITION

YOUR INNER GPS
CONNECTING TO YOUR INTUITION

....
....
....
....
....
....
....
....
....
....
....
....
....
....
....
....
....
....
....
....
....
....

WEEKLY REFLECTION:

self care & wellness	career & business
finance	family & friends
physical environment	self development

....
....
....
....
....
....
....

YOUR GOALS FOR THIS WEEK:

make sure to double check to stay in alignment
with monthly goals

self care & wellness	career & business
finance	family & friends
physical environment	self development

....

....

....

....

....

....

week: | your intention for this week:

YOUR TOP 3 PRIORITIES TODAY:

	mon	tues	wed
1.			
2.			
3.			

YOUR BLESSINGS TODAY:

what will you no longer hold on to this week?

	thur	fri	sat/ sun
1.			
2.			
3.			

YOUR BLESSINGS TODAY:

♡ ☐ ☐ ☐   ♡ ☐ ☐ ☐   ♡ ☐ ☐ ☐

YOUR INNER GPS
CONNECTING TO YOUR INTUITION

YOUR INNER GPS
CONNECTING TO YOUR INTUITION

WEEKLY REFLECTION:

self care & wellness	career & business
finance	family & friends
physical environment	self development

....

....

....

....

....

....

....

YOUR GOALS FOR THIS WEEK:

make sure to double check to stay in alignment
with monthly goals

self care & wellness	career & business
finance	family & friends
physical environment	self development

....

....

....

....

....

....

....

....

....

....

....

....

....

....

....

....

....

....

....

....

week:	your intention for this week:

YOUR TOP 3 PRIORITIES TODAY:

	mon	tues	wed
1.			
2.			
3.			

YOUR BLESSINGS TODAY:

♡ ☐ ☐ ☐   ♡ ☐ ☐ ☐   ♡ ☐ ☐ ☐
☐ ☐ ☐   ☐ ☐ ☐   ☐ ☐ ☐
☐ ☐ ☐   ☐ ☐ ☐   ☐ ☐ ☐

what will you no longer hold on to this week?

	thur	fri	sat/ sun
1.			
2.			
3.			

YOUR BLESSINGS TODAY:

YOUR INNER GPS
CONNECTING TO YOUR INTUITION

YOUR INNER GPS
CONNECTING TO YOUR INTUITION

WEEKLY REFLECTION:

self care & wellness	career & business
finance	family & friends
physical environment	self development

....

....

....

....

....

....

....

MONTHLY REFLECTION

WOW! You've just completed the first month of your 6-month transformation journey, and that is a huge achievement!
You've shown up for yourself, embraced new habits, and taken the first powerful steps toward creating lasting change. This is only the beginning, and there's so much more growth and success ahead.

On the following pages, I invite you to reflect on this first month. What goals did you set at the start? How have you begun to shift and grow in these early stages? What have you learned about yourself? Celebrate every small win and recognize how far you've already come on your path to personal transformation.

This month wasn't just about checking off tasks—it was about laying the foundation for your self-development and success. The habits you've started to build and the insights you've gained are planting the seeds for your future success.

And guess what? This is just the start! The journey ahead is filled with even more opportunities for personal growth, self-discovery, and confidence building. As you move into the next month, keep building on your momentum. Stay committed to your journaling practice, your reflections, and your goals.

You are limitless, and the more you keep showing up for yourself, the more you'll realize how much you're truly capable of. Keep going—you've only just scratched the surface of what's possible!

MONTHLY REFLECTION:

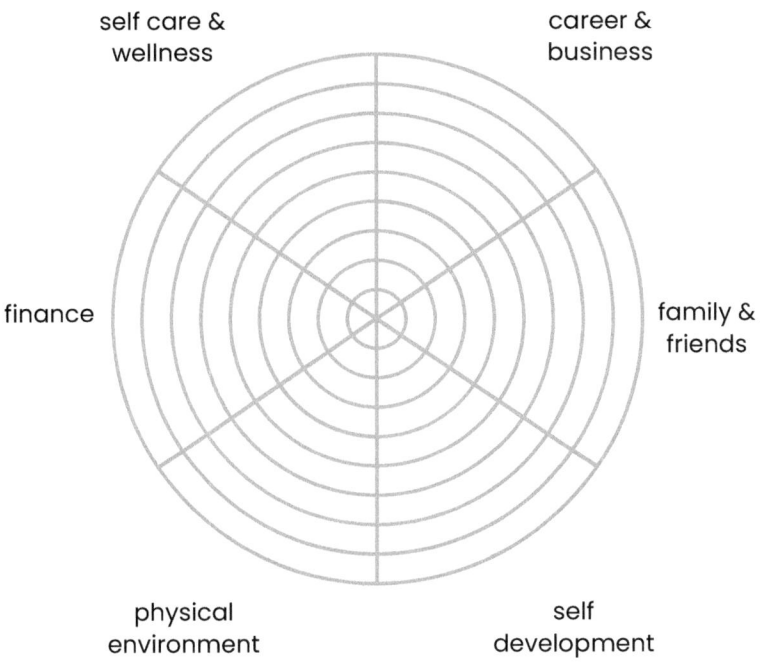

self care & wellness

career & business

finance

family & friends

physical environment

self development

Just like with your first inventory wheel, the following pages give you space to go deeper into each area of your life. Be honest and open—the more honest you are, the more clarity and growth you'll experience.

self care & wellness

....

....

....

....

....

career & business

....

....

....

....

....

finance

....

....

....

....

....

family & friends

....

....

....

....

....

....

physical environment

....

....

....

....

....

....

self development

....

....

....

....

....

....
....
....
....
....
....
....
....
....
....
....
....
....
....
....

MONTHLY GOALS PROCESS BAR

how far did I come so far? track your progress right
here
(and don´t forget to be proud of yourself!) :

O————————————O————————————O

ADDITIONAL JOURNALING

MONTH 4

THE KEY TO HAVING IT ALL IS KNOWING
you deserve it.

YOUR 3 GOALS FOR THIS MONTH

(in alignment with your main goals):

goal:

the action(s) you will
take to achieve them:

1.

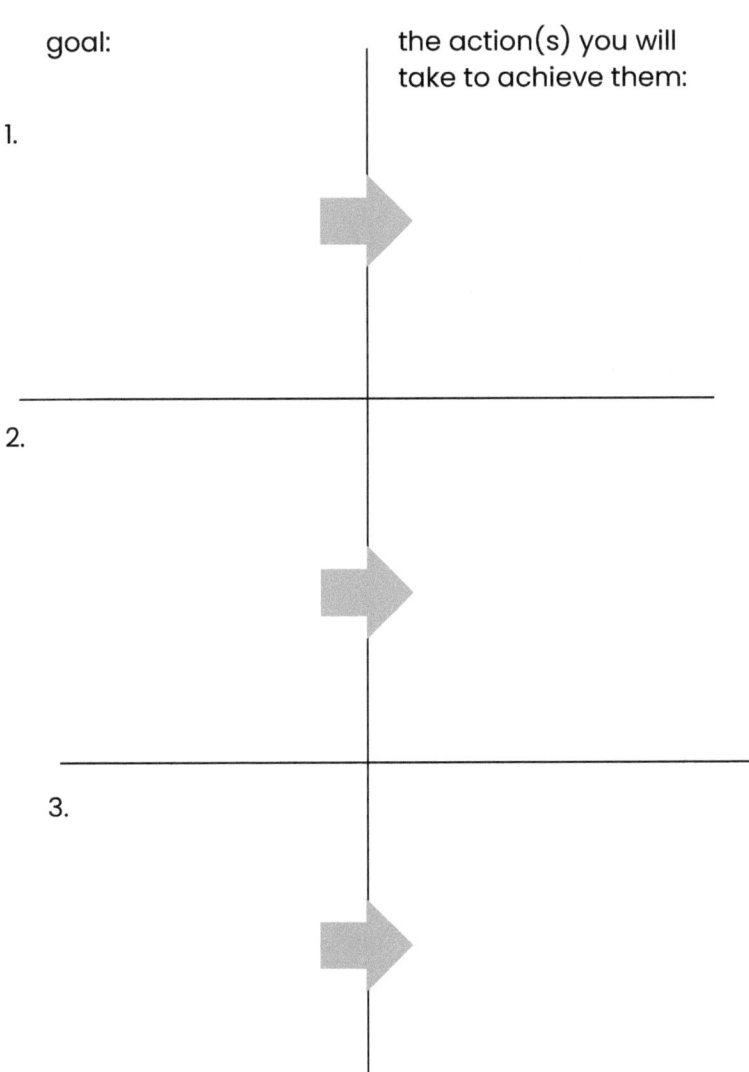

2.

3.

YOUR GOALS FOR THIS WEEK:

make sure to double check to stay in alignment
with monthly goals

self care & wellness	career & business
finance	family & friends
physical environment	self development

....

....

....

....

....

....

YOUR INNER GPS
CONNECTING TO YOUR INTUITION

YOUR INNER GPS
CONNECTING TO YOUR INTUITION

....
....
....
....
....
....
....
....
....
....
....
....
....
....
....
....
....
....
....
....
....
....

WEEKLY REFLECTION:

self care & wellness	career & business
finance	family & friends
physical environment	self development

....

....

....

....

....

....

....

YOUR GOALS FOR THIS WEEK:

make sure to double check to stay in alignment
with monthly goals

self care & wellness	career & business
finance	family & friends
physical environment	self development

....

....

....

....

....

....

week:	your intention for this week:

YOUR TOP 3 PRIORITIES TODAY:

	mon	tues	wed
1.			
2.			
3.			

YOUR BLESSINGS TODAY:

♡ ☐ ☐ ☐   ♡ ☐ ☐ ☐   ♡ ☐ ☐ ☐
⟨♥⟩ ☐ ☐ ☐   ⟨♥⟩ ☐ ☐ ☐   ⟨♥⟩ ☐ ☐ ☐
💰 ☐ ☐ ☐   💰 ☐ ☐ ☐   💰 ☐ ☐ ☐

what will you no longer hold on to this week?

	thur	fri	sat/ sun
1.			
2.			
3.			

YOUR BLESSINGS TODAY:

YOUR INNER GPS
CONNECTING TO YOUR INTUITION

YOUR INNER GPS
CONNECTING TO YOUR INTUITION

WEEKLY REFLECTION:

self care & wellness	career & business
finance	family & friends
physical environment	self development

....

....

....

....

....

....

....

....

....

....

....

....

....

....

....

....

....

....

....

....

....

....

....

....

....

....

....

....

....

....

YOUR GOALS FOR THIS WEEK:

make sure to double check to stay in alignment
with monthly goals

self care & wellness	career & business
finance	family & friends
physical environment	self development

....

....

....

....

....

....

week: | your intention for this week:

YOUR TOP 3 PRIORITIES TODAY:

	mon	tues	wed
1.			
2.			
3.			

YOUR BLESSINGS TODAY:

♡ ☐ ☐ ☐   ♡ ☐ ☐ ☐   ♡ ☐ ☐ ☐
🏋 ☐ ☐ ☐   🏋 ☐ ☐ ☐   🏋 ☐ ☐ ☐
💰 ☐ ☐ ☐   💰 ☐ ☐ ☐   💰 ☐ ☐ ☐

what will you no longer hold on to this week?

	thur	fri	sat/ sun
1.			
2.			
3.			

YOUR BLESSINGS TODAY:

♡ ☐ ☐ ☐   ♡ ☐ ☐ ☐   ♡ ☐ ☐ ☐
☐ ☐ ☐   ☐ ☐ ☐   ☐ ☐ ☐
☐ ☐ ☐   ☐ ☐ ☐   ☐ ☐ ☐

YOUR INNER GPS
CONNECTING TO YOUR INTUITION

YOUR INNER GPS
CONNECTING TO YOUR INTUITION

WEEKLY REFLECTION:

self care & wellness	career & business
finance	family & friends
physical environment	self development

....

....

....

....

....

....

....

YOUR GOALS FOR THIS WEEK:

make sure to double check to stay in alignment
with monthly goals

self care & wellness	career & business
finance	family & friends
physical environment	self development

....

....

....

....

....

....

week: | your intention for this week:

YOUR TOP 3 PRIORITIES TODAY:

	mon	tues	wed
1.			
2.			
3.			

YOUR BLESSINGS TODAY:

what will you no longer hold on to this week?

	thur	fri	sat/ sun
1.			
2.			
3.			

YOUR BLESSINGS TODAY:

YOUR INNER GPS
CONNECTING TO YOUR INTUITION

YOUR INNER GPS
CONNECTING TO YOUR INTUITION

....

....

....

....

....

....

....

....

....

....

....

....

....

....

....

....

....

....

....

....

....

WEEKLY REFLECTION:

self care & wellness	career & business
finance	family & friends
physical environment	self development

....
....
....
....
....
....
....

MONTHLY REFLECTION

WOW! You've just completed the first month of your 6-month transformation journey, and that is a huge achievement!
You've shown up for yourself, embraced new habits, and taken the first powerful steps toward creating lasting change. This is only the beginning, and there's so much more growth and success ahead.

On the following pages, I invite you to reflect on this first month. What goals did you set at the start? How have you begun to shift and grow in these early stages? What have you learned about yourself? Celebrate every small win and recognize how far you've already come on your path to personal transformation.

This month wasn't just about checking off tasks—it was about laying the foundation for your self-development and success. The habits you've started to build and the insights you've gained are planting the seeds for your future success.

And guess what? This is just the start! The journey ahead is filled with even more opportunities for personal growth, self-discovery, and confidence building. As you move into the next month, keep building on your momentum. Stay committed to your journaling practice, your reflections, and your goals.

You are limitless, and the more you keep showing up for yourself, the more you'll realize how much you're truly capable of. Keep going—you've only just scratched the surface of what's possible!

MONTHLY REFLECTION:

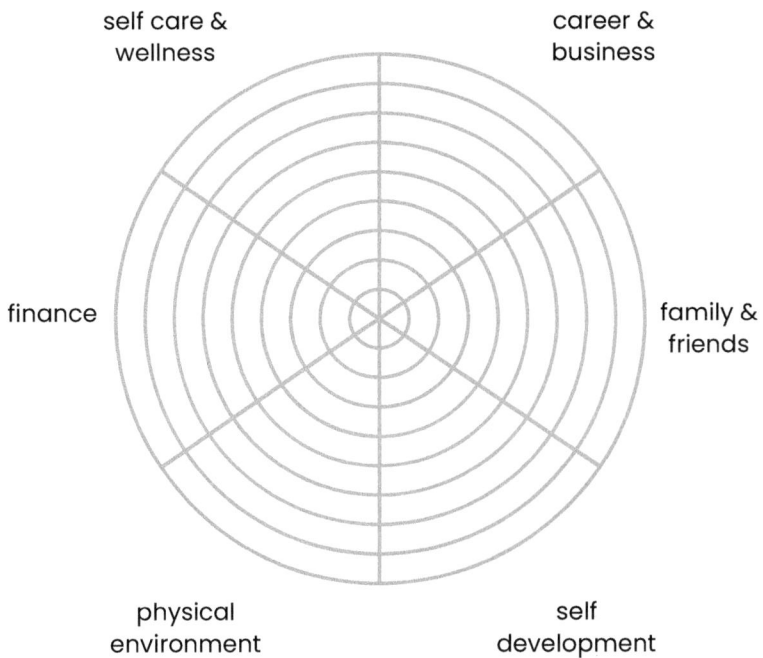

self care &
wellness

career &
business

finance

family &
friends

physical
environment

self
development

Just like with your first inventory wheel, the following pages give you space to go deeper into each area of your life. Be honest and open—the more honest you are, the more clarity and growth you'll experience.

self care & wellness

....

....

....

....

....

....

career & business

....

....

....

....

....

....

finance

....

....

....

....

....

family & friends

....

....

....

....

....

....

physical environment

....

....

....

....

....

....

self development

....

....

....

....

....

....
....
....
....
....
....
....
....
....
....
....
....
....
....

MONTHLY GOALS PROCESS BAR

how far did I come so far? track your progress right
here
(and don´t forget to be proud of yourself!) :

◯——————————◯——————————◯

ADDITIONAL JOURNALING

MONTH 5

THE BEST REVENGE
IS TO
TAKE AWAY YOUR ATTENTION AND
be happy.

YOUR 3 GOALS FOR THIS MONTH

(in alignment with your main goals):

goal:

the action(s) you will
take to achieve them:

1.

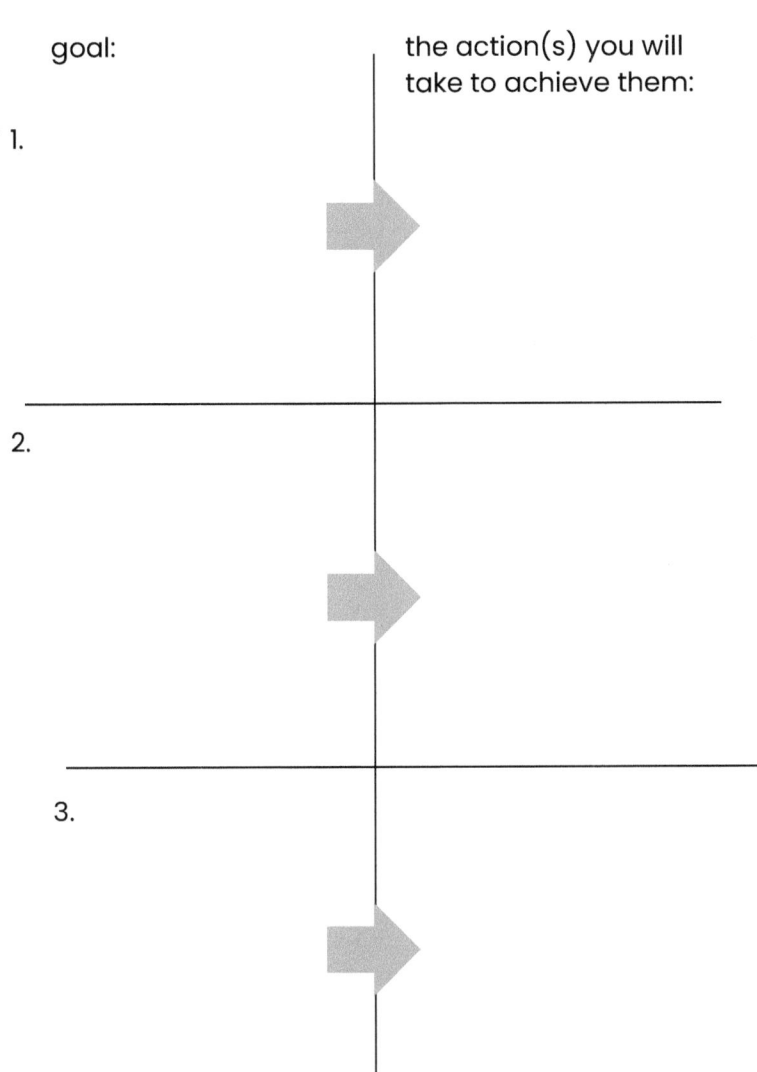

2.

3.

YOUR GOALS FOR THIS WEEK:

make sure to double check to stay in alignment
with monthly goals

self care & wellness	career & business
finance	family & friends
physical environment	self development

....

....

....

....

....

....

YOUR INNER GPS
CONNECTING TO YOUR INTUITION

YOUR INNER GPS
CONNECTING TO YOUR INTUITION

....
....
....
....
....
....
....
....
....
....
....
....
....
....
....
....
....
....
....
....
....

WEEKLY REFLECTION:

self care & wellness	career & business
finance	family & friends
physical environment	self development

....

....

....

....

....

....

....

YOUR GOALS FOR THIS WEEK:

make sure to double check to stay in alignment
with monthly goals

self care & wellness	career & business
finance	family & friends
physical environment	self development

....

....

....

....

....

....

week:

your intention for this week:

YOUR TOP 3 PRIORITIES TODAY:

mon	tues	wed

1.

2.

3.

YOUR BLESSINGS TODAY:

♡ ☐ ☐ ☐   ♡ ☐ ☐ ☐   ♡ ☐ ☐ ☐
♥ ☐ ☐ ☐   ♥ ☐ ☐ ☐   ♥ ☐ ☐ ☐
☐ ☐ ☐ ☐   ☐ ☐ ☐   ☐ ☐ ☐

what will you no longer hold on to this week?

	thur	fri	sat/ sun
1.			
2.			
3.			

YOUR BLESSINGS TODAY:

YOUR INNER GPS
CONNECTING TO YOUR INTUITION

YOUR INNER GPS
CONNECTING TO YOUR INTUITION

....
....
....
....
....
....
....
....
....
....
....
....
....
....
....
....
....
....
....
....

WEEKLY REFLECTION:

self care & wellness	career & business
finance	family & friends
physical environment	self development

....

....

....

....

....

....

....

YOUR GOALS FOR THIS WEEK:

make sure to double check to stay in alignment
with monthly goals

self care & wellness	career & business
finance	family & friends
physical environment	self development

....

....

....

....

....

....

| week: | your intention for this week: |

YOUR TOP 3 PRIORITIES TODAY:

	mon	tues	wed
1.			
2.			
3.			

YOUR BLESSINGS TODAY:

♡ ☐ ☐ ☐   ♡ ☐ ☐ ☐   ♡ ☐ ☐ ☐
☐ ☐ ☐   ☐ ☐ ☐   ☐ ☐ ☐
☐ ☐ ☐   ☐ ☐ ☐   ☐ ☐ ☐

what will you no longer hold on to this week?

	thur	fri	sat/ sun
1.			
2.			
3.			

YOUR BLESSINGS TODAY:

YOUR INNER GPS
CONNECTING TO YOUR INTUITION

YOUR INNER GPS

CONNECTING TO YOUR INTUITION

....
....
....
....
....
....
....
....
....
....
....
....
....
....
....
....
....
....
....

WEEKLY REFLECTION:

self care & wellness	career & business
finance	family & friends
physical environment	self development

....

....

....

....

....

....

....

YOUR GOALS FOR THIS WEEK:

make sure to double check to stay in alignment
with monthly goals

self care & wellness	career & business
finance	family & friends
physical environment	self development

....

....

....

....

....

....

....

....

....

....

....

....

....

....

....

....

....

....

....

....

....

....

....

....

....

YOUR TOP 3 PRIORITIES TODAY:

	mon	tues	wed
1.			
2.			
3.			

YOUR BLESSINGS TODAY:

what will you no longer hold on to this week?

thur	fri	sat/ sun

1.

2.

3.

YOUR BLESSINGS TODAY:

♡ ☐ ☐ ☐   ♡ ☐ ☐ ☐   ♡ ☐ ☐ ☐
☐ ☐ ☐   ☐ ☐ ☐   ☐ ☐ ☐
☐ ☐ ☐   ☐ ☐ ☐   ☐ ☐ ☐

YOUR INNER GPS
CONNECTING TO YOUR INTUITION

YOUR INNER GPS
CONNECTING TO YOUR INTUITION

....

....

....

....

....

....

....

....

....

....

....

....

....

....

....

....

....

....

....

....

....

WEEKLY REFLECTION:

self care & wellness	career & business
finance	family & friends
physical environment	self development

....

....

....

....

....

....

....

MONTHLY REFLECTION

WOW! You've just completed the first month of your 6-month transformation journey, and that is a huge achievement!
You've shown up for yourself, embraced new habits, and taken the first powerful steps toward creating lasting change. This is only the beginning, and there's so much more growth and success ahead.

On the following pages, I invite you to reflect on this first month. What goals did you set at the start? How have you begun to shift and grow in these early stages? What have you learned about yourself? Celebrate every small win and recognize how far you've already come on your path to personal transformation.

This month wasn't just about checking off tasks—it was about laying the foundation for your self-development and success. The habits you've started to build and the insights you've gained are planting the seeds for your future success.

And guess what? This is just the start! The journey ahead is filled with even more opportunities for personal growth, self-discovery, and confidence building. As you move into the next month, keep building on your momentum. Stay committed to your journaling practice, your reflections, and your goals.

You are limitless, and the more you keep showing up for yourself, the more you'll realize how much you're truly capable of. Keep going—you've only just scratched the surface of what's possible!

MONTHLY REFLECTION:

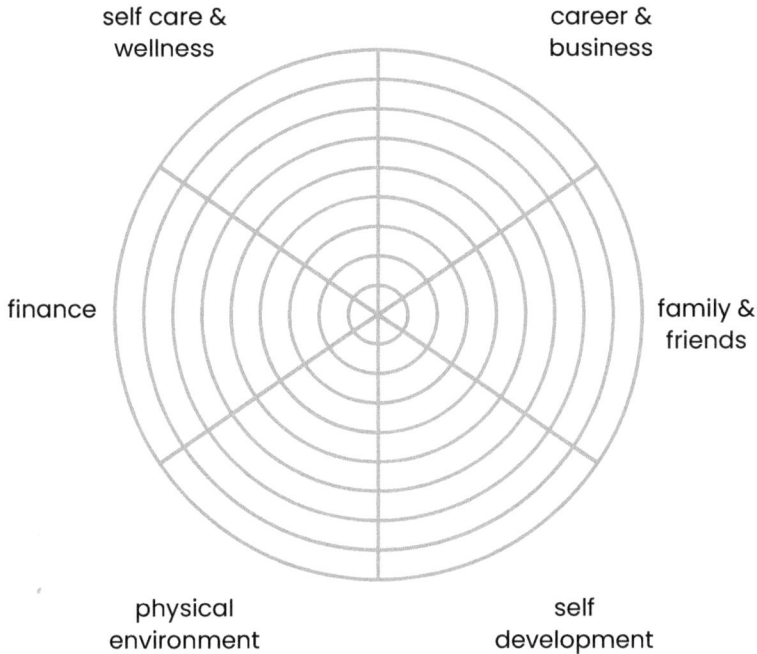

self care & wellness

career & business

finance

family & friends

physical environment

self development

Just like with your first inventory wheel, the following pages give you space to go deeper into each area of your life. Be honest and open—the more honest you are, the more clarity and growth you'll experience.

self care & wellness

....

....

....

....

....

....

career & business

....

....

....

....

....

....

finance

....

....

....

....

....

family & friends

....

....

....

....

....

....

physical environment

....

....

....

....

....

....

self development

....

....

....

....

....

....
....
....
....
....
....
....
....
....
....
....
....
....
....

MONTHLY GOALS PROCESS BAR

how far did I come so far? track your progress right here
(and don´t forget to be proud of yourself!) :

O————————————————O————————————————O

ADDITIONAL JOURNALING

MONTH 6

The secret
of your future
is hidden

IN YOUR
ROUTINES.

YOUR 3 GOALS FOR THIS MONTH

(in alignment with your main goals):

goal:

the action(s) you will
take to achieve them:

1.

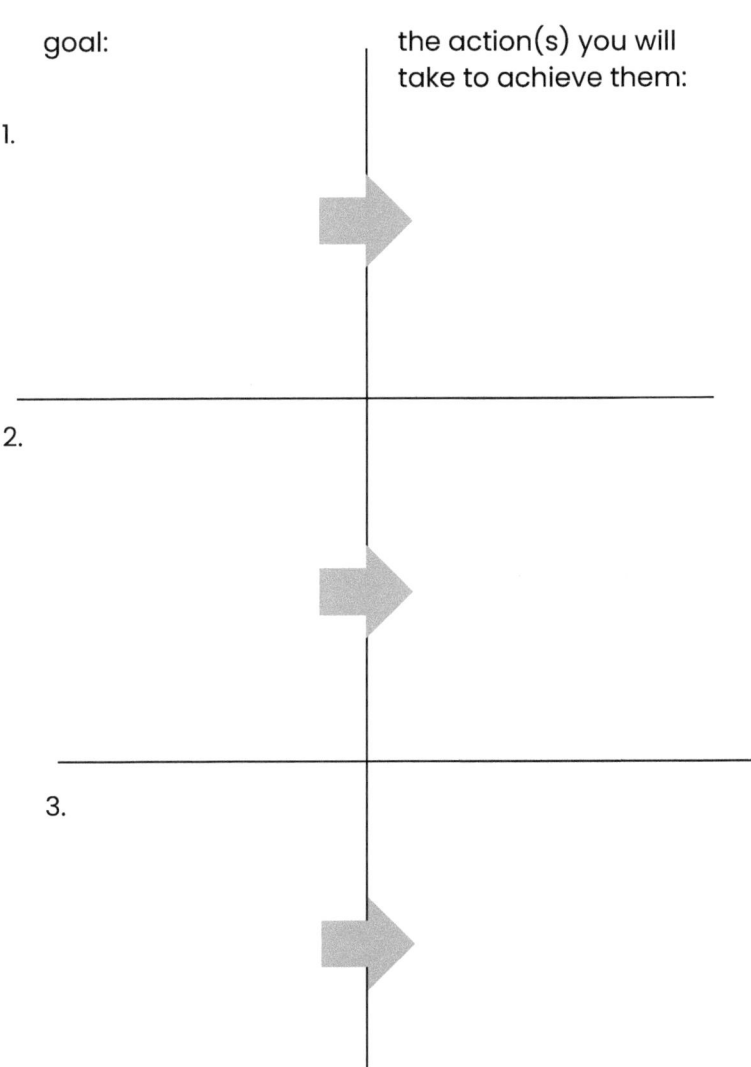

2.

3.

YOUR GOALS FOR THIS WEEK:

make sure to double check to stay in alignment
with monthly goals

self care & wellness	career & business
finance	family & friends
physical environment	self development

....

....

....

....

....

....

YOUR INNER GPS
CONNECTING TO YOUR INTUITION

YOUR INNER GPS
CONNECTING TO YOUR INTUITION

....
....
....
....
....
....
....
....
....
....
....
....
....
....
....
....
....
....
....
....

WEEKLY REFLECTION:

self care & wellness	career & business
finance	family & friends
physical environment	self development

....

....

....

....

....

....

....

YOUR GOALS FOR THIS WEEK:

make sure to double check to stay in alignment
with monthly goals

self care & wellness	career & business
finance	family & friends
physical environment	self development

week: _____ | your intention for this week:

YOUR TOP 3 PRIORITIES TODAY:

	mon	tues	wed
1.			
2.			
3.			

YOUR BLESSINGS TODAY:

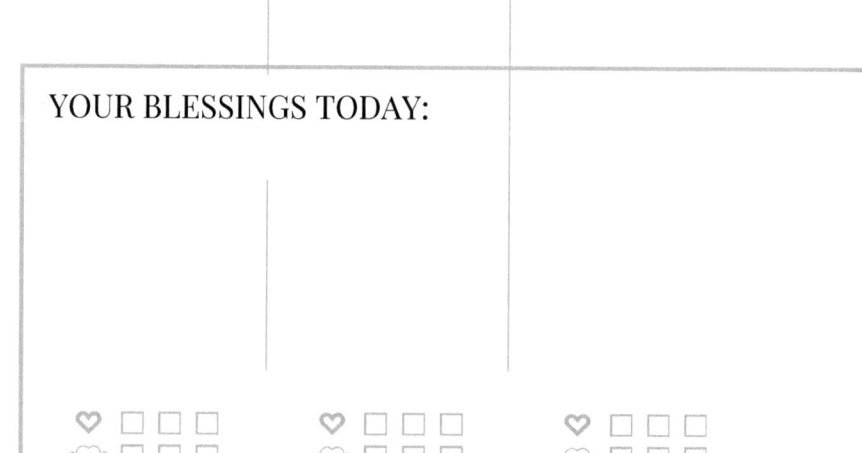

what will you no longer hold on to this week?

	thur	fri	sat/ sun
1.			
2.			
3.			

YOUR BLESSINGS TODAY:

♡ ☐ ☐ ☐   ♡ ☐ ☐ ☐   ♡ ☐ ☐ ☐
☐ ☐ ☐   ☐ ☐ ☐   ☐ ☐ ☐
☐ ☐ ☐   ☐ ☐ ☐   ☐ ☐ ☐

YOUR INNER GPS
CONNECTING TO YOUR INTUITION

YOUR INNER GPS
CONNECTING TO YOUR INTUITION

....

....

....

....

....

....

....

....

....

....

....

....

....

....

....

....

....

....

....

WEEKLY REFLECTION:

self care & wellness	career & business
finance	family & friends
physical environment	self development

YOUR GOALS FOR THIS WEEK:

make sure to double check to stay in alignment
with monthly goals

self care & wellness	career & business
finance	family & friends
physical environment	self development

....

....

....

....

....

....

week:	your intention for this week:

YOUR TOP 3 PRIORITIES TODAY:

	mon	tues	wed
1.			
2.			
3.			

YOUR BLESSINGS TODAY:

♡ ☐ ☐ ☐   ♡ ☐ ☐ ☐   ♡ ☐ ☐ ☐

☐ ☐ ☐   ☐ ☐ ☐   ☐ ☐ ☐

☐ ☐ ☐   ☐ ☐ ☐   ☐ ☐ ☐

what will you no longer hold on to this week?

	thur	fri	sat/ sun
1.			
2.			
3.			

YOUR BLESSINGS TODAY:

♡ ☐ ☐ ☐   ♡ ☐ ☐ ☐   ♡ ☐ ☐ ☐
☐ ☐ ☐   ☐ ☐ ☐   ☐ ☐ ☐
☐ ☐ ☐   ☐ ☐ ☐   ☐ ☐ ☐

YOUR INNER GPS
CONNECTING TO YOUR INTUITION

YOUR INNER GPS
CONNECTING TO YOUR INTUITION

....

....

....

....

....

....

....

....

....

....

....

....

....

....

....

....

....

....

WEEKLY REFLECTION:

self care & wellness	career & business
finance	family & friends
physical environment	self development

....

....

....

....

....

....

....

YOUR GOALS FOR THIS WEEK:

make sure to double check to stay in alignment
with monthly goals

self care & wellness	career & business
finance	family & friends
physical environment	self development

....

....

....

....

....

....

week:

your intention for this week:

YOUR TOP 3 PRIORITIES TODAY:

mon	tues	wed

1.

2.

3.

YOUR BLESSINGS TODAY:

♡ ☐ ☐ ☐   ♡ ☐ ☐ ☐   ♡ ☐ ☐ ☐

☐ ☐ ☐   ☐ ☐ ☐   ☐ ☐ ☐

☐ ☐ ☐   ☐ ☐ ☐   ☐ ☐ ☐

what will you no longer hold on to this week?

	thur	fri	sat/ sun
1.			
2.			
3.			

YOUR BLESSINGS TODAY:

♡ ☐ ☐ ☐   ♡ ☐ ☐ ☐   ♡ ☐ ☐ ☐
⟨♡⟩ ☐ ☐ ☐   ⟨♡⟩ ☐ ☐ ☐   ⟨♡⟩ ☐ ☐ ☐
☗ ☐ ☐ ☐   ☗ ☐ ☐ ☐   ☗ ☐ ☐ ☐

YOUR INNER GPS
CONNECTING TO YOUR INTUITION

YOUR INNER GPS
CONNECTING TO YOUR INTUITION

WEEKLY REFLECTION:

self care & wellness	career & business
finance	family & friends
physical environment	self development

....

....

....

....

....

....

....

MONTHLY REFLECTION

WOW! You've just completed the first month of your 6-month transformation journey, and that is a huge achievement!
You've shown up for yourself, embraced new habits, and taken the first powerful steps toward creating lasting change. This is only the beginning, and there's so much more growth and success ahead.

On the following pages, I invite you to reflect on this first month. What goals did you set at the start? How have you begun to shift and grow in these early stages? What have you learned about yourself? Celebrate every small win and recognize how far you've already come on your path to personal transformation.

This month wasn't just about checking off tasks—it was about laying the foundation for your self-development and success. The habits you've started to build and the insights you've gained are planting the seeds for your future success.

And guess what? This is just the start! The journey ahead is filled with even more opportunities for personal growth, self-discovery, and confidence building. As you move into the next month, keep building on your momentum. Stay committed to your journaling practice, your reflections, and your goals.

You are limitless, and the more you keep showing up for yourself, the more you'll realize how much you're truly capable of. Keep going—you've only just scratched the surface of what's possible!

MONTHLY REFLECTION:

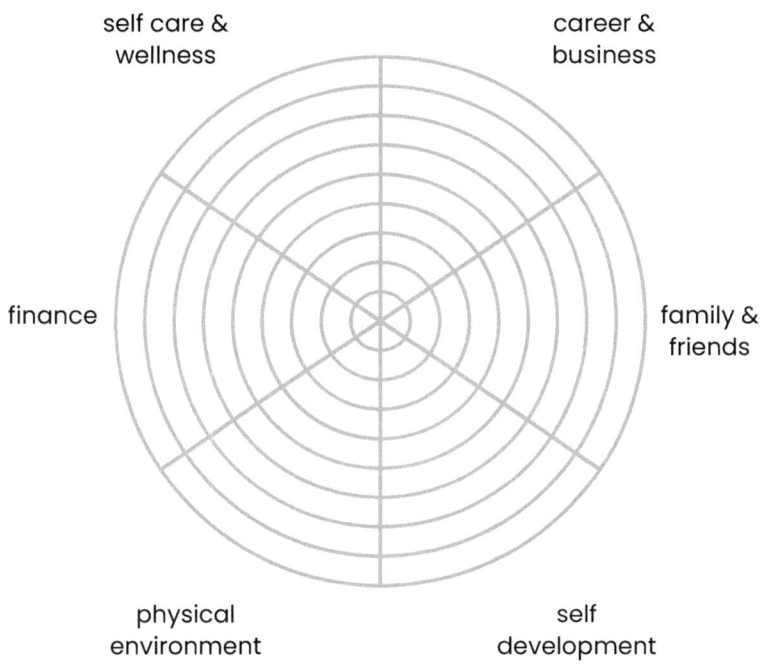

self care &
wellness

career &
business

finance

family &
friends

physical
environment

self
development

Just like with your first inventory wheel, the following
pages give you space to go deeper into each area of
your life. Be honest and open—the more honest you
are, the more clarity and growth you'll experience.

self care & wellness

....

....

....

....

....

....

career & business

....

....

....

....

....

....

finance

....

....

....

....

....

family & friends

....

....

....

....

....

....

physical environment

....

....

....

....

....

....

self development

....

....

....

....

....

....

....

....

....

....

....

....

....

....

....

....

....

....

....

....

MONTHLY GOALS PROCESS BAR

how far did I come so far? track your progress right here
(and don't forget to be proud of yourself!) :

○————————————————○————————————————○

ADDITIONAL JOURNALING

ADDITIONAL JOURNALING

6-MONTH REFLECTION

OH MY GOODNESS! YOU MADE IT!

Take a moment to really let that sink in—you just completed an entire 6 months of transformation! THAT IS MASSIVE! You've committed, shown up for yourself, and proven that you have everything it takes to create lasting change. This is a moment worth celebrating!

On the following pages, I invite you to reflect deeply on where you started. What were your goals 6 months ago? Have they evolved as you've grown, or stayed the same? How close have you come to achieving those goals, and how have you surprised yourself along the way?

You didn't just go through the motions—these 6 months, doing this journal you've embraced new habits, gained insights, and unlocked levels of self-awareness and growth you may not have thought possible before.

I have no doubt that by completing this 6-month transformation, you've fallen in love with the daily journaling routines, and the weekly and monthly reflections that have become such a powerful part of your life. And guess what? The best part is that this journey doesn't end here! You can take everything you've learned and dive into your next 6 months, continuing to build on your progress and reach new heights of transformation.

You are limitless. Your growth has no ceiling. The possibilities are endless when you commit to showing up for yourself every single day.

Please tag @TheKathrineLouis on your socials when you share your incredible achievements and where you are in your journey—I am beyond excited to witness your continued transformation and celebrate with you. Together, we are building a community of empowered women who are showing the world what's possible. We are all SO proud of you!

This is just the beginning of what you're capable of. Keep going, keep growing, and know that the best is yet to come.
Remember, You Can. And Will. create a life you love!

Happy transformation!

With so much love and pride,
Kathrine Louis

YOUR GOALS:

the goals you
set:

the goals you
achieved:

"old" you

"transformed" you

YOUR 6-MONTH REFLECTION:

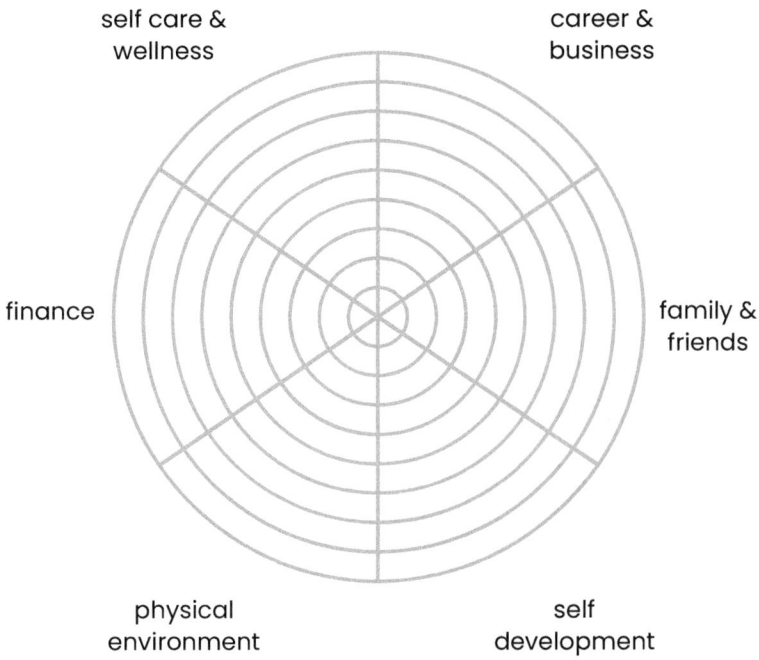

self care &
wellness

career &
business

finance

family &
friends

physical
environment

self
development

Use these pages to dive deep into each area of your
life and compare it to your very first inventory.
Embrace the transformation—see how far you've
come, how much you've grown, and let it ignite your
excitement for all the possibilities ahead!

self care & wellness

....

....

....

....

....

career & business

....

....

....

....

....

finance

....

....

....

....

....

family & friends

....

....

....

....

....

....

physical environment

....

....

....

....

....

....

self development

....

....

....

....

....

....
....
....
....
....
....
....
....
....
....
....
....
....
....
....
....

6 MONTHS GOALS PROCESS BAR

how far did I come so far? track your progress right here
(and don´t forget to be proud of yourself!) :

○————————————————○————————————————○

MY 6-MONTH REFLECTION:

....

....

....

....

....

....

....

....

....

....

....

....

....

....

....

....

....

....

....

ADDITIONAL JOURNALING

ADDITIONAL JOURNALING

ADDITIONAL JOURNALING

ADDITIONAL JOURNALING

....

....

....

....

....

....

....

....

....

....

....

....

....

....

....

....

....

....

....

....

....

....

....

ADDITIONAL JOURNALING

ADDITIONAL JOURNALING

EPILOGUE

I wrote this journal for you—for every woman who feels like the life she's living doesn't quite align, as though something is missing or out of place. I wrote it for my younger self, for all those days when she felt lost and stuck in the wrong place.

It took me years to discover who my best self truly is, and even longer to step into her fully. But I want you to take the shortcut! I want you to benefit from the lessons I've learned over the past two decades and apply them to your own journey.

The techniques in this journal are designed to make that transformation possible for you.
For extra support, visit www.KathrineLouis.com/Meditations for exclusive guided meditations to elevate your self-worth. And don't forget to check out www.KathrineLouis.com for your free Audio Training on productivity and to sign up for my newsletter, Sunday Mail, for exclusive behind-the-scenes insights and support.
If you've been enjoying "Finally Becoming Her" and want to support me, please leave a ☆☆☆☆☆ review on Amazon or wherever you purchased your copy. Your feedback means the world to me and would be an incredible support as a first-time author. Thank you so much in advance!

Remember, this is your life—your one and only life. You deserve every dream, every desire, and every ounce of happiness you've ever envisioned.
"You Can. And You Will." create a life you truly love.